MARKETING YOUR PRODUCT

101 for
SMALL BUSINESS

MARKETING YOUR PRODUCT

Donald Cyr, MBA
Douglas Gray, LLB

Self-Counsel Press
(a division of)
International Self-Counsel Press Ltd.
USA   Canada

Self-Counsel Press acknowledges the financial support of the Government of Canada through the Book Publishing Industry Development Program (BPIDP) for our publishing activities.

Printed in Canada.

First edition: 1987
Reprinted: 1988; 1989; 1991
Second edition: 1994
Reprinted: 1994
Third edition: 1998
Fourth edition: 2003
Fifth edition: 2009

Library and Archives Canada Cataloguing in Publication Data

Cyr, Donald G.

    Marketing your product / Donald Cyr, Douglas Gray. — 5th ed.
    ISBN 978-1-55180-859-8

1. Marketing. 2. Small business. I. Gray, Douglas A. II. Title.
HF5415.G73 2009   658.8   C2009-903136-1

Mixed Sources
Product group from well-managed forests, controlled sources and recycled wood or fiber
www.fsc.org Cert no. SW-COC-000952
© 1996 Forest Stewardship Council

FSC

Self-Counsel Press
(a division of)
International Self-Counsel Press Ltd.

1704 N. State Street
Bellingham, WA 98225
USA

1481 Charlotte Road
North Vancouver, BC V7J 1H1
Canada

CONTENTS

5 RESEARCHING YOUR MARKET

14 MANAGING IN A COMPETITIVE WORLD

15 SELLING AS A MARKETING TECHNIQUE

18 LEGAL CONSIDERATIONS

APPENDIXES

TABLES

SAMPLES

WORKSHEETS

To Ruth, special thanks for your support and contribution.

D.C.

To Diana, my wife, friend, and intrepid entrepreneur,
for her constant encouragement
und enthusiasm.

D.G.

ACKNOWLEDGMENTS

We would like to thank Mr. Wayne Karlowsky, MBA, for his contribution to Appendix 1, Researching Your Market.

Mr. Karlowsky has 18 years' experience as a senior marketer, national director at Wellington Insurance, and vice president at Angus Reid Group Inc., a market research and polling company. As president of Nonsuch Communications, he is now actively involved in developing and implementing marketing strategies for his own company.

INTRODUCTION

The marketing needs of small businesses are unique and vary considerably from those of corporations. Many large corporations operate on a highly structured basis; whole departments may be devoted to developing and implementing comprehensive marketing plans using extensive resources of money, time, and personnel.

A typical small business usually lacks this sophistication.

Marketing is both an art and a science. As an art, it involves creativity and insight. As a science, it involves planning, analysis, and discipline. You need to learn how to combine and balance both art and science to maximize the potential of your company and capitalize on the strengths of your personnel.

This book is designed as a practical, step-by-step guide for the small-business person. It will assist you in maximizing your available resources by providing practical marketing

strategies that work for small business. The text provides general theory and advice, and the appendixes provide worksheets for developing your personalized marketing plan.

Chapter 1 gives you an overview of product marketing. In Chapters 2 to 5 you will learn how to market and plan strategically, how to segment your market and identify consumer behavior, and how to apply market research techniques that work. Next, in Chapters 6 to 9, you will learn how to develop your product, price it effectively, and advertise and promote it. How to get your product to your customer is covered in Chapter 10, and for those of you involved in retail marketing, we have included Chapter 11 to point out the special marketing considerations for that type of merchandising.

Chapter 12 discusses marketing your product on the Internet. Chapters 13 and 14 discuss the competitive edge and management in a competitive world. Selling is an essential part of marketing and is discussed in Chapter 15. In Chapter 16, tips for implementing your marketing plan are given, including advice on setting and staying on schedule and how to get back on course if you stray. Chapter 17 discusses marketing your product internationally. Finally, in Chapter 18, we deal with the legal problems you may encounter in product marketing and give tips on how to avoid some common pitfalls. Also, look for the question section at the end of most chapters. These are designed to help you focus on key issues.

This book combines the practical insights of small business marketers with the experience of consulting and academic marketing professionals. If you follow the guidelines and tips outlined and complete the worksheets in this book, you should enjoy increased profits and your customers should be more satisfied with you and your product. We wish you success in your marketing endeavors.

Note: This book attempts to highlight business and marketing concepts and techniques accurately. However, the information is general, and no legal, tax, or financial advice is given.

If legal or other expert advice is required, you should obtain the services of competent professionals.

1
WHAT IS MARKETING?

1. Marketing

Remember when "Made in Japan" implied an inexpensive, poor-quality product? Today, many Japanese products are recognized as high-quality industry leaders. This change in perception is due to effective marketing. Many people consider marketing simply as pricing gimmicks, advertising, and hard-sell. On the contrary, marketing is an essential management function needed to create a demand for your product. The core concept of marketing is the exchange of value between two parties: the buyer and the seller. This means that in your marketing planning, your primary functions are to —

(a) understand the needs and desires of present and potential customers,

(b) select and develop products that best satisfy those customers within the limits of your resources,

(c) develop a program to tell your customers about the benefits of your product, and

(d) ensure that your products get to your customer.

1.1 Understanding customer needs and desires

We all tend to assume that others' needs are the same as our own. Understanding your customers means finding out what they really want, and recognizing that their needs and desires may be very different from your own. Market research can reduce the uncertainty and risk of deciding what products you should present. Marketing does not try to impose a product that is not required or wanted. Effective marketing is user-oriented, not seller-oriented.

1

1.2 Selecting and developing a product

A marketing-oriented business does not attempt to be all things to all people. Once you have identified the needs and characteristics of several markets, decide which one to serve on the basis of profit potential, market size, and your company's goals and available resources. Each market will be different, so you have to design diffcrent product benefits to meet each market requirement.

1.3 Developing a communication program

Once you develop appropriate products for your different markets, you must decide how to communicate the benefits of each product. You might use promotion, advertising, personal selling, public relations, and media selection. All these marketing tools are explored in this book.

1.4 Getting your product to your customer

Getting your product to your customer means offering your product at the right place, at the right time, and at the right price. It means making it easy for your customer to find and buy your product.

2. Marketing Mix

Four variables make up the marketing mix: product, price, place, and promotion. You as a businessperson can control, vary, and use these variables to influence your customers.

These variables are interrelated and form the total package that will determine the degree of your marketing success. Following is a brief description of the four variables; each is discussed in detail in later chapters.

2.1 Product

A product is designed to satisfy consumer needs. Product strategy includes decisions about its uses, quality, features, brand name, style, packaging, guarantees, design, and options. Decisions about changes in the product characteristics are needed as the product goes through its life cycle (see Chapter 6).

2.2 Price

Besides being the amount you charge customers for your product, price involves management policies on discounts, allowances, credit terms, payment periods, transit payments, etc.

2.3 Place

Placing your product means providing it at the right place at the right time. Distribution strategies involve decisions on such things as store location and territories, inventory levels, shelf location, and type of shipments.

2.4 Promotion

Promotion is informing and persuading your target market of the value of your product. The major promotional tools are advertising, personal selling, publicity, and sales promotion. Which media you use is also an important part of promotion.

3. Selling versus Marketing

Despite the rhetoric of catering to customer needs and solving problems, sales-oriented organizations have traditionally consisted of talkative salespeople trying to foist their products on customers. Don't you make that mistake!

The marketing-oriented organization seeks to make a profit by serving the needs of customers and solving their problems. The marketing concept is concerned with the fair exchange of value between the consumer and the organization. Marketing is different from sales in that you first determine the customer's needs and then design a product or service to satisfy those needs.

Marketing is really about listening to your customer. In a sales-oriented organization, salespeople listen with the intent to reply; marketers listen with the intent to understand.

Inventing a product without first checking if it is needed is similar to having your optometrist give you his or her personal eyeglass prescription without first examining your own eyes. In a marketing-oriented organization, your first priority is to find out if a product is needed before offering it.

In a marketing-oriented organization, the sales manager's responsibilities relate mainly to the following:

(a) Determining sales objectives

(b) Establishing a sales force size and structure

(c) Formulating sales implementation programs

(d) Recruiting, training, and supervising the sales force

(e) Formulating a motivating compensation package

(f) Setting budget and sales expenses

(g) Developing sales forecasts

(h) Establishing ties between the different functional groups

(i) Evaluating sales representatives

A sales representative has many responsibilities ranging from simply taking orders to building goodwill, trade selling, prospecting, and negotiating contracts. Personal characteristics that are required include empathy, patience, persuasive ability, and persistence. The stereotypical image of a sales representative is of an extroverted, joke-telling socialite trying to foist his or her product on you. But the best salespeople take the time to listen to a client's needs and provide solutions to fit those needs.

4. Product versus Service Marketing

Although product marketing has much in common with service marketing, the strategy is not the same. Services are performed and consumed while products are manufactured and possessed. The following service sector attributes are different from those of the product sector:

(a) Services are intangible, which makes it difficult for the consumer to inspect the services before purchase. Services cannot be displayed, physically demonstrated, or illustrated in the same manner as a product. For example, unlike products such as books or cameras, legal services cannot be seen, felt, tasted, smelled, or touched before they are bought. Because consumers can see few physical attributes prior to the purchase, they may feel there is a greater risk associated with the selection of a service.

(b) Services are simultaneously consumed and produced. The person rendering the service requires the consumer to be present throughout the service delivery. For example, medical examinations, beauty salons, and travel tours all take place with both the customer and agent present. This characteristic limits the scale of a service operation to the number of qualified personnel available. Regardless of the size of the office, a dentist can treat only so many patients per hour.

(c) The quality of a service is affected by the client's own input. A psychiatrist, doctor, or psychologist requires the patient's cooperation. A management consultant's advice depends on the client's honest disclosure of information in order for the recommendations to be appropriate and effective.

(d) Services cannot be inventoried because most are performed by people. Empty seats in an airplane or unused electric power represents lost business and cannot be stored for the next day.

(e) Services are not standardized; the quality of service varies depending on where and when it is performed. For example, different sales representatives in a travel agency have varying levels of experience. Depending on the expertise of the sales representative you use, you may or may not be advised of the most economical travel package. In the product arena, however, machines ensure standardization. In a service organization, the quality and consistency of service is highly dependent on the person giving the service.

5. Avoiding Failure; Ensuring Success

Statistics vary, but the majority of new products fail. Studies indicate that 75 percent of product failures can be attributed to poor marketing. In order of priority, the most common reasons for product failure are the following:

(a) *Misunderstanding the market:* Failure to properly analyze market needs and habits leads to a poor understanding of the benefits your customer was looking for. You must be careful not to assume that what you want to offer is what your customer wants.

(b) *Product quality:* The quality, value, and performance of your product may not meet your customers' expectations or may be inferior to the competition.

(c) *Lack of marketing effort:* Failure to provide the required training, support, and follow-up for an effective marketing effort erodes the commitment and team effort critical to the success of any business.

(d) *Poor planning:* Failure to set realistic goals, objectives, and tasks often leads to higher costs than anticipated, which in turn results in a higher price. Higher prices often mean lower sales volumes. It is common to over-estimate the revenue and underestimate the cost of bringing a product to market.

(e) *Competition:* The competition's quick reaction to copy and improve on your product or overcrowd the market could force you out of business.

(f) *Failure to adapt:* Not revising goals, maintaining inflexible attitudes, arrogance or overconfidence, and unanticipated obstacles can lead to failure. Adaptability and ongoing reassessment of your goals is practical and realistic.

(g) *Lack of technical competence:* Not assessing your strengths and weaknesses, or marketing a product you are unfamiliar with or do not have technical competence or production expertise in, can lead to failure.

This book provides many practical tips and information that will contribute to the success of your business. As you read on, keep in mind the four main reasons why a product succeeds:

(a) *Use of an effective marketing approach:* Answering the basic marketing questions and acting on that information is essential to the success of your product. Stay in touch with your customers; find out what they really need and want and where you stand in the market.

(b) *Have a unique product:* Most successful products are either superior to and/or different from those of the competition. Successful businesses care about product quality and the services they provide.

(c) *Technical competence:* Have technical competence in the production or distribution of your product. Gain knowledge and experience in the industry and a "hands-on" understanding of what is happening. Provide meaningful rewards to employees for good work.

(d) *Competitive pricing:* Are your prices competitive compared to similar products? Do you offer added value? Do you have sufficient margins to cover your costs and give incentive to your distributors?

2

MARKETING PLANNING, GOAL-SETTING, AND STRATEGY

Marketing strategy identifies the current position of your business and sets short- and long-term goals for the future. Without a strategic marketing plan, marketing efforts are likely to be reactive rather than proactive.

Strategic planning can be described as a method for achieving an end by anticipating the future and determining the course of action required. Planning requires that a business recognize where it is now, where it would like to be, and how it proposes to get there. A marketing plan is a working document you and others in your business will use and review on an ongoing basis. It is not an abstract treatise you develop and then put on the shelf.

A marketing plan is meant to be used to measure how you are doing, where you have been, and what needs to be done differently in the future. It is not cast in concrete when written, but is a flexible working document. Most marketing plans are revised annually. Your business may change quickly, generating a need to supplement it quarterly or semi-annually with more specific action plans.

Each section of your company should plan their objectives annually; each section's plans should be consistent with your overall company strategy. A marketing plan helps you make decisions on such things as media selection, promotion, advertising, distribution, product development and related services, personnel requirements, training, and expenditures for the coming year.

Note: Portions of this chapter have been drawn from *Marketing Your Service* by Jean Withers and Carol Vipperman, another title in the Self-Counsel business series.

1. Understanding the Planning Process

Companies today operate in a dynamic environment. A change to that environment creates both opportunities and problems. The rest of this chapter reviews the main stages in the strategic planning and goal-setting process that allow a company to adapt to changing conditions and take advantage of new opportunities.

1.1 Situation analysis: "Where are we now?"

As a marketing planner, you must recognize that your business, in relation to competing businesses, has strengths upon which strategies should be based and weaknesses that should be avoided. To assess your company's resources and to determine your position in relation to the competition, answer the following questions:

Product

- Who is your customer?

- What is the demand for your product?

- Is the demand stable or cyclical?

- How big is your market?

- How often do customers use your product?

- Is your product used only in association with other products? Can your product, therefore, be a substitute?

- Is your product durable? The demand for durable products, such as appliances, varies with construction cycles.

- Is your product a necessity or luxury? Fluctuation in income offsets demand for luxury goods.

- What stage of the life cycle is your product in? If it is in the mature stage, does it need modification? (See Chapter 6 for a discussion of a product's life cycle.)

- Do you hold a patent on your product? (Or can it be copied by the competition?)

- How is your product perceived by your customers, by the community, and by your competitors?

- Do you have information systems to provide you with reports on your customers?

- What written information about your product is available for your customers?

Personnel

- What is your attitude toward growth, profit maximization, and market penetration?

- Are employees underqualified or overqualified?

- What incentives exist for rewarding personnel for sales, training, or promotion?

- Do you have employees with the required technical expertise? Are you paying equal, more, or less than the industry norm? Is your commission fee realistic?

Financial strength

- Does the cost per unit decrease the more you produce? Does your business require a large initial capital outlay?

- What is your investment mix? How much money comes from profit, shareholders, or commercial lenders?

- What is your expected rate of return?

- What are the risks of your present investments?

- How much do you have in accounts receivable?

- What is the aged spread of your receivables?

- What are your credit terms? Are they too generous?

- What is your cost of capital?

- Can you obtain money when you need it?

Facilities

- What is the cost of material? Do supplies fluctuate? Do prices fluctuate?

- Is your source of supplies dependable? Do other sources exist?

- Can you substitute materials for products?

- Is your office size, plant size, or outlet size adequate?

- Is your equipment critical? Does it need to be replaced? Is it flexible?

1.2 Identifying problems and opportunities

Ask yourself, "What does the future hold?" Having established your strengths and weaknesses, you must now align your company strengths with market opportunities. The environment outside your business is in constant flux. Changing cultural values, technology, demographics, legal regulations, economics, public opinion, and competitor strategy can all create opportunities for or threats to your organization. Based on your strengths and these external trends, you must decide how to best take advantage of market opportunities.

2. Formulating Goals

Having analyzed the company situation and its environment, you are now in a position to shape the direction and operation of your business. Marketing objectives should be consistent with your company objectives and missions.

You need to set clear goals to identify what tasks are required, when they need to be done, and who is responsible for accomplishing them. Monitoring your marketing strategy is much easier when clear responsibilities, tasks, and objectives have been defined.

After marketing problems are recognized and marketing opportunities are identified, most people are able to decide what they want to achieve. Setting marketing goals is simply the process of laying the pathway to the future.

The field of psychology has amply demonstrated the power of goals for individuals. When people set goals, they gain clarification and direction. When people achieve goals, they gain a measure of success and confidence in the future. Without goals, people lose interest in life.

Businesses must have a focus. You must be prepared to live with your goals when you achieve them. For example, if your goal is to increase sales significantly and sell 1,000,000 widgets next year, then you must be prepared to spend more on advertising, hire more salespeople, find more storage space for widgets, or find another way to achieve your goal. You must be prepared to make any changes necessary to live with the achievement of your goals.

2.1 What are goals, anyway?

Simply stated, goals are the long-term results you want your business to achieve. When writing your goals, remember the following:

- Goals are broad, sweeping statements.

- Goals are both realistic (so they can be achieved) and challenging (so you must strive to achieve them).

- Goals may be set for your personal or business life or for each element in the marketing mix.

- Goals may overlap; therefore, they should be integrated.

2.2 Clarifying goals

Clarity of personal and business goals is an essential foundation of marketing goals. For example, these might be the life and business goals of one retailer:

- *A general life goal:* To balance all parts of my life, career, family, and friends.

- *A general business goal:* To have competitors respect me as a professional.

The company and marketing goals might be dramatically influenced by your personal goals:

- *A general company goal:* To be earning a net profit of $xxx annually by 20--. (That net profit would be affected by your wish to spend time pursuing other aspects of life that provide balance.)

- *A general marketing goal:* To establish and secure the west coast as our primary market. (Instead of, perhaps, choosing a national market or national prominence because of previous commitments.)

3. Your Personal and Company Goals

Once you understand the importance of knowing your own goals, it is essential that you clarify them and state them specifically. Let the following guide you as you set the goals:

- *Be honest* with yourself. Ultimately your own wishes, not those of others, dictate what you achieve. Future achievements will come most comfortably if based on honest assumptions now.

- *Be passionate* about these goals. Passion is a word applied too infrequently in business. And in the clear, cool logic of developing any business plan, passion

may seem inappropriate. But if you don't care deeply, the drive to achieve goals is missing.

- *Be realistic* about what is genuinely possible. This is important when integrating diverse business goals. For example, a goal of increasing sales significantly without increasing the staff may not be possible. Maturity becomes most important when integrating business goals with personal choices. For some, the price of dedication to family, other interests, and even humanity would be inordinately high. If this is the case, you must adjust your sights.

- *Keep your perspective.* Goals are not irrevocably set. They can be changed, modified, or removed. They arc a tool to use at will in business.

- *Visualize your goals.* Anticipate what success will look like and feel like as a rehearsal for achieving goals. As you're setting each goal, ask yourself: "Can I see it?" If not, can you help yourself see it in time? Almost any businessperson who has the discipline to succeed can certainly create the mental image that creates achievement.

Use the planning worksheets in the appendixes to record your personal and business goals.

To set your company's goals, look five years into the future. What do you see? Where do you want to be? Write it down.

Think about the stepping stones to your goal. What are the interim goals necessary to achieve that five-year goal? For example, if you want to sell your product in international markets in Year Five, what must you do in Years Four, Three, Two, and within the next year, Year One, to make it happen?

To achieve the five-year goal, build on the foundation as follows. Within the next year, focus on strengthening the markets you already have. Particularly, begin to build up expertise in the markets you want to develop.

In Year Two, begin to make contacts internationally and do marketing studies to test the feasibility of your plan. In Year Three, you might do a test and try to sell your product to a controlled group within the international market. In Year Four, expand your test market while maintaining your stronghold at home. By Year Five, your goal should be achieved.

Setting and integrating your goals requires time and thought. It won't and shouldn't come easily.

4. Setting Objectives

4.1 Why goals are never enough

Although goals are a guide for creating the future, they lack the immediacy that would help achieve them. Goals don't necessarily assure success.

In business, you must specify *when* you will do *how much of what* to achieve the goal; that is, set objectives.

4.2 The role of objectives

Ideally, objectives generate the urgency that is needed to inspire you to achieve a goal. In practice, your objectives also present the best solution to problems identified in the firm. Objectives both inspire and provide solutions if they have the following three characteristics:

(a) They are *specific and measurable.*

(b) They are achievable within a *limited time.*

(c) They are identified with an actual *result.*

Determining the result to be achieved sometimes creates confusion. Some businesspeople try to be too specific about how the objectives will be achieved when they should really be concerned with what will be achieved.

4.3 What does a typical objective look like?

Make your product available to more buyers. Fulfill more customer needs. Expand or change your product's distribution. Build customer acceptance in a new market or for a new product. Increase total dollar sales per customer. These are typical marketing objectives.

Objectives focus further attention on the following six marketing elements:

(a) Service

(b) Price

(c) Place or way product is distributed

(d) Promotion

(e) Customers to be served

(f) Sales

Where writing marketing goals is an exercise in vision, writing marketing objectives is an exercise in discipline. From the broadly drawn sketch of goals is rendered a detailed and precise portrait. Here are some examples of marketing objectives that are specific and time-bound, and that have a measurable end result.

4.3.a Product objectives

Introduce [*how many*] new products by [*specific date*]. Improve [*name of product*] by [*making which specific change*] before [*specific date*].

4.3.b Price objectives

Raise prices [*amount*] on [*specific date*] so they are within [*percentage*] of similar products.

4.3.c Place objectives

Penetrate the [*city or defined region*] area more deeply by developing [*amount*] contracts by [*date*].

Move offices to a more appropriate [*amount*] square foot location in [*general area*] by [*date*].

4.3.d Promotion objectives

Increase awareness about the product before [*date*].

4.3.e Customer objectives

Provide [*type*] service to [*specific type of customers*] by [*date*].

4.3.f Sales objectives

Sell [*definite amount*] by [*specific date*]. Increase the average order size to [*dollar value*] sales by [*date*].

5. Integrating Goals and Objectives

To march forward into the future, you must set objectives that mesh with the goals you want to achieve. For example, a promotion goal of increasing the market's awareness of your product's image must be integrated with promotion objectives that specify developing an effective brochure or flyer by the end of the year and selling ten percent more products within six months.

Your task now is to integrate the marketing goal you want to achieve next year with the *how much*, *what*, and *when* required to achieve it. Use the worksheets in the appendixes to record the objectives that will lead you to your marketing goals.

6. Planning Your Specific Strategy

Using your company's strengths to take advantage of the opportunities in the marketplace is good strategy. Strategy is concerned with where a company should be headed in the future and the major moves to be taken to ensure its success.

There are many approaches to planning a company strategy. One method compares market attractiveness to business strength to help evaluate opportunities.

Market attractiveness is the appeal of the product to potential customers. How big is the market? Is it growing? What image does the product convey? Is the market changing its values and attitudes toward the product? How would a change in technology affect your product?

Business strength is your company's position within your market. What is your market share? Do you charge more, less, or a similar price to that of your competition? Are customer perceptions easily influenced by a change in price? What level of service do you provide? How does it compare and how important is service to product sales? Are you in a position to react quickly and effectively to competitors' challenges? How well do you really know your customer? Is high turnover a problem with your sales staff?

To determine where market opportunities exist, evaluate each product separately for its market attractiveness and business strength as either strong, medium, or weak. When there are many strong factors in both categories, then there are many opportunities in the marketplace for that product.

6.1 Evaluating alternatives

Once you have selected a market to serve, you must then decide if you will serve one segment of the target market or a combination of segments. (Segmentation and positioning are explained in more detail in Chapter 4.)

Market segmentation recognizes that, within a market, there are differences among potential customers. In segmenting, you divide the market into homogeneous submarkets and tailor your marketing mix to appeal only to that segment. The strategy is to offer a unique appeal and to establish your company as distinct from its competitors.

In appealing to a combination of segments, you can build up the size of your target market. A combination offers a marketing mix with general appeal rather than having a different marketing mix for each segment. The strategy is not to satisfy everyone but to satisfy enough people to make a profit. Combination works best where there is little product differentiation. Lightbulbs, for example, are perceived as virtually the same no matter what the brand name is.

6.2 Designing your action plan

The primary emphasis and objective of strategic thinking is to determine *what* should be done. The action plan needs to decide *how much*, *when*, and *who* is going to do *what*.

First, you need to define the marketing program and break it into separate tasks. This allows you to focus your full attention on the work that needs to be done. An advertising campaign for a special sales promotion may be divided into selecting which merchandise to promote, ensuring that enough merchandise is available, writing the advertising copy, preparing the layout, selecting the media, scheduling ads and sales, deciding where in the store the merchandise will be displayed, and the type of display wanted.

Second, note the sequence and relationships of parts. For example, the length of copy and the layout depends on the type of media used. Sequence is critical in other cases such as making sure the sales merchandise and point of purchase display are in place before you advertise. List the tasks in logical order.

Third, decide who is responsible for carrying out each task. In many organizations, task function will be part of a routine operation.

Fourth, decide how each part will be done and the resources required. If the resources are not available, you may decide that the objectives are beyond your business's capacity. You may have to modify, reduce, or alter your objectives and redefine your strategy to fit your available resources.

Finally, estimate the time and cost of each step. The schedule should show starting dates, completion dates, and the cost for each task tabulated.

6.3 Monitoring system

A monitoring system is a periodic review to evaluate if the firm's marketing plan is meeting its marketing goal. The monitoring system can spot lack of coordination or skills, or poor strategies. Monitoring should find out what is happening and why. If necessary, corrective action can then be taken to improve performance and capitalize on the things done well.

Note: See Appendix 3 for a full description of what should be in your marketing plan. To help you analyze your company and your marketing goals, complete the questions on the following pages.

1. YOUR MARKETING GOALS

1. What is important to you personally and in your business?

_____

_____

_____

_____

2. How much time does each aspect of life require of you?

_____

_____

_____

_____

3. What are your lifetime business goals?

_____

_____

_____

_____

4. How would you like to spend the next three to five years in your business?

_____

_____

_____

_____

5. If you knew you would die six months from today, how would you spend your time until then?

_____

_____

_____

_____

6. What are your company goals for the next —
   (a) five years?

   _____

   _____

   _____

   _____

   (b) four years?

   _____

   _____

   _____

   _____

   (c) three years?

   _____

   _____

   _____

   _____

   (d) two years?

   _____

   _____

   _____

   _____

   (e) one year?

   _____

   _____

   _____

   _____

7. Think of your goals for the next year. What are your specific goals for —
   (a) your products?

   _____

   _____

   _____

   _____

(b) your prices?

_____

_____

_____

(c) your location?

_____

_____

_____

_____

(d) the way the product is promoted?

_____

_____

_____

_____

(e) your customers?

_____

_____

_____

_____

_____

(f) the sales the company will generate?

_____

_____

_____

_____

8. Summarize your company's general and marketing goals.

_____

_____

_____

_____

_____

_____

2. YOUR MARKETING OBJECTIVES

1. Write down your marketing objectives in a specific and measurable way. (Your objectives represent desired results and need to be compatible with your company goals and market environment demands.) What are your specific marketing objectives for —

(a) your product?

_____

_____

_____

_____

(b) your price?

_____

_____

_____

_____

(c) your location?

_____

_____

_____

_____

(d) the way the product is promoted?

_____

_____

_____

_____

(e) your clients?

_____

_____

_____

_____

(f) the sales the company will generate?

_____

_____

_____

_____

2. Under what assumptions are your objectives attainable? (Stipulate what operational and external conditions or factors will allow you to obtain your objective.)

_____

_____

_____

_____

_____

3. What marketing tools do you plan to use to reach your customer? (Elaborate on each tool you want to use: product development, promotional campaign, distribution system, price structure.)

_____

_____

_____

_____

_____

_____

_____

4. Elaborate on each of the following:

(a) Tasks and responsibilities. (Who will do what?)

_____

_____

_____

_____

_____

_____

(b)   Assign deadlines for each part of your marketing plan that you want to implement in the first six months. (Specify tasks and start and finish dates.)

_____

_____

_____

_____

_____

_____

_____

_____

(c)   List the above tasks in order of priority.

_____

_____

_____

_____

_____

_____

_____

_____

(d)   What special coordination is needed to complete each task? Which departments need to be involved?

_____

_____

_____

_____

_____

_____

_____

_____

5. If your plan fails due to unpredictable factors, what is your alternate strategy?

_____
_____
_____
_____
_____
_____
_____
_____
_____

3. EXTERNAL INFLUENCES

1. How do current economic conditions affect your firm? What are some expected economic changes?

_____
_____
_____
_____
_____
_____
_____
_____
_____
_____

2. Do you know of any expected technological advances in your industry? What are they?

_____
_____
_____
_____
_____
_____
_____

3. Are there any changes in the law that could affect your business? What are they and how would they affect your business?

_____
_____
_____
_____
_____
_____

4. Could a change in the political climate affect your business and marketing strategy? How?

_____
_____
_____
_____
_____
_____
_____
_____

5. Are there any special interest groups, agencies, media personnel, or other agencies that could have a positive or negative impact on your business?

_____
_____
_____
_____
_____
_____

6. Who are your competitors? Describe their customers.

_____
_____
_____
_____
_____
_____

7. Are income levels in the community stable? Is the population base stable or seasonal?

_____

_____

_____

_____

4. INTERNAL INFLUENCES

1. What are your firm's strengths and weaknesses?

_____

_____

_____

_____

_____

_____

_____

_____

2. Is your operating budget consistent with your plan? If not, what adjustments can you make?

_____

_____

_____

_____

_____

3. Does the nature of your operation require some type of credit for your customer? On what criteria will you grant credit?

_____

_____

_____

_____

_____

5. CUSTOMER ANALYSIS

1. Is the person buying your product the same one who wants and uses it?

    _____
    _____
    _____
    _____
    _____
    _____

2. How do customers learn about your product (e.g., advertising, salespeople, friends, relatives)?

    _____
    _____
    _____
    _____
    _____

3. Which sources of information are the most influential? Why?

    _____
    _____
    _____
    _____
    _____
    _____

4. Do your customers buy out of habit?

    _____
    _____
    _____
    _____

5. Is your customer's buying decision influenced by his or her family, friends, or colleagues?

    _____
    _____
    _____
    _____
    _____

6. Are you aware how your customers feel after they use your product? What do customers seem to like best about your product? What don't they like?

_____

_____

_____

_____

_____

_____

_____

7. Will your customers buy your product again?

_____

_____

_____

_____

_____

_____

_____

8. Do most customers buy on weekends, evenings?

_____

_____

_____

_____

_____

_____

9. Where do people currently buy similar products?

_____

_____

_____

_____

_____

_____

3
THE MARKETING ENVIRONMENT

Luck comes to those who are prepared. In marketing, being in the right place at the right time means being in tune with your marketing environment.

The marketing environment consists of major social forces that you cannot control, but which affect your company's ability to operate effectively and profitably. The marketing environment is continually changing and you need to adapt your business to take advantage of opportunities and avoid threats.

There are five major marketing environmental forces: demographics, technology, culture, economics, and politics. Changes in any one of these represent opportunities or threats to a company. Marketing strategies must be aligned with marketing environment changes and continually revised. To be prepared, you must constantly monitor the marketing environment. Let's briefly review each major marketing environmental force and its implications for marketing strategy.

1. Demographics

Demographics are the statistical characteristics of your market. They include its size, age distribution, family composition, ethnic mix, mobility, and geographical distribution.

A shift in population, such as the birthrate decline that started in 1964, is both an opportunity and a threat. Johnson & Johnson, which originally sold a line of baby shampoo, oil, and powder responded to the decline in birthrate by promoting its products to adults. Johnson & Johnson turned a potential problem into an opportunity.

To other industries such as hotels, restaurants, and airlines, a lower birthrate represents opportunity because smaller families mean more time and income for traveling and dining out.

Recently, the states surrounding the Rockies — Montana, Idaho, Wyoming, Utah, Colorado, and New Mexico — have replaced California as the new American heartland. Low crime, fresh air, beautiful scenery, and old, backcountry values have attracted the new cowboy — the young, professional telecommuter.

Due to downsizing from corporate restructuring, and easy access through data communication, computers, and fax machines, the Rockies have attracted new residents: high-tech managers. The shift to the Rockies will increase the demand for housing and household goods. As well, it represents opportunities for local companies that sell furniture, gardening tools, and cooking equipment. It means high profits to astute companies that cater to the new lifestyle.

An aging population means lower motorcycle sales but a higher demand for quality clothes. The increased number of immigrants from countries where the extended family is an integral part of tradition, means that salespeople have to adapt their style to suit families as opposed to individuals. Changing family composition and better-educated consumers are other demographic social forces that companies need to monitor.

2. Technology

A customer's only loyalty is to a better product. Exceptions exist, but how many people do you know who still use a slide rule or abacus for calculations, watch black and white television, or use a carbon copy instead of a photocopy? A change in technology can have rapid and drastic effects on entire industries.

Keeping track of new technology leads to product innovations and new systems that can help you operate more effectively and efficiently.

New technology may mean lower production costs, more efficient inventory control, and better management information systems. Lower production costs mean you can charge a lower price and gain a greater market share. Efficient inventory control means better product delivery to customers. A better management information system allows you to make better decisions about what price to charge, what product to offer, or which advertising campaign creates the greatest impact. New technology needs to be complemented with a knowledge-based work force to gain a competitive advantage.

You need to keep track of new technology if you want your business to survive. However, new technology, like research, must be evaluated for its benefits. Does it improve product quality, help lower production costs, or improve your information system and help you make better decisions? Technology that improves customer service is an investment. Any other type of technology is a cost.

Technology needs to be used to serve customers better. Hotel and airline computer reservation systems, voice mail, library electronic search systems, and remote control devices are examples of innovations designed to serve people better. A yearning for the "good old days" is a longing for a time when human relations were more important than technology or mechanical systems. Technology should add to your customer service, not detract from it.

Management needs to create a positive attitude toward change. Project members should be rewarded for their success. You need to tolerate mistakes and provide a sense of security. Many managers may resent losing the authority they gained with years of service. Insistence on the right answer, rules, and procedures discourages creativity. A respect for education, a highly skilled staff, and interaction with outsiders is conducive to the acceptance of new ideas.

3. Culture

Society forms our beliefs and values, and shapes the standards that govern how we relate to people. As a society, North Americans are highly influenced by such values as freedom, individuality, practicality, achievement, progress, humanitarianism, comfort, youthfulness, and health. As a value, practicality supports products that work well and save time, while individualism favors the acceptance of unique products that fit one's personality. It is important to adapt products to the cultural values held by consumers and for marketers to constantly monitor changes in values that may affect business.

In North America there are major subcultures based on differences in geographical area, religion, age, and ethnic background. Baby boomers, baby busters, and seniors are examples of different age groups that have different values.

3.1 Baby boomers

In the 1980s, society's consumption patterns were largely influenced by the baby boomers (i.e., people born between 1946 and 1964). Parents of baby boomers lived through the Great Depression in the 1930s and saw the post-World War II boom. Their attitude toward spending was one of restraint and they saved their money and paid cash for what they wanted rather than buying on credit. The boomers were raised during a more prosperous period and developed liberal spending habits and a happy-go-lucky attitude toward credit.

As one-third of the population, and 44 percent of the heads of households, the baby boomers are now reaching their highest earning potential. When the boomers were young, they had good purchasing power. They created the consumption binge of the 1980s. Now, as the boomers begin to gray, they shoulder responsibility for their children and their aging parents. The dog-eat-dog world of the 1990s has given way to a focus on noncareer issues and a search for values. The "me" generation is now less concerned with showing off. They want something that makes them feel good. They want to treat themselves to luxury hotels and gourmet dining. With the great number of middle-aged boomers in established relationships, personal happiness and the desire to become more spontaneous and informal are becoming more important. The boomers are increasingly searching for goods that provide the following:

(a) *Health:* Products and services that foster wellness, low-fat food, exercise equipment, cosmetics, and fashionable clothing adapted to the chic graying market.

(b) *Time:* With both men and women working, leisure time has been reduced. Time is money and any product or service that can save time is valuable. Convenience foods, fast check-out and delivery, and lasting, reliable products are important.

(c) *Home:* Many men and women dissatisfied with work are seeking greater intimacy and enjoyment from being at home. Home building supplies, home entertainment goods, and home decorative accessories are important.

(d) *Environment:* The boomer search for things natural makes them highly sensitive to environmentally friendly products. Look for limited phosphate content in detergents, recyclable products, and reduced packaging.

(e) *Leisure:* The puritan work ethic is now accompanied by the notion of a balance between work, home, and recreation.

Recreation is seen as an expression of self. Mountain bikes, scuba diving gear, ski equipment, and do-it-yourself kits and books are now popular. The bathroom was once considered a purely utilitarian space. Now it is common to find designer bathroom fixtures, whirlpool baths, soaker tubs, and exercise equipment in the bathroom. Gourmet kitchens and trekking equipment represent marketing opportunities to satisfy the increasing need for a feeling of well-being by consumers.

(f) *Advertising:* The "me" generation is shifting to a "we" society. Advertising focus is shifting away from pure self-indulgence toward sharing. The boomers' mistrust of authority means they are less likely to take things at face value. Pertinent information that accurately describes your product is required.

The materialism that marked the 1980s is giving way to added value. Added value is not necessarily related to expense but rather to selected quality, convenience, and comfort. Consumption focuses on quality. Instead of buying three pairs of shoes, many buy one good pair.

Overall trends don't apply to everyone. Marketers need to recognize that different segments of consumers have different needs. Within each segment, cultural value shifts take place. Opportunities exist for those businesses that adapt their marketing strategies to the cultural shift within their segments.

3.2 Generation Y

Generation Y (people born 1979-1994) share much with boomers. They both want flexibility in the workplace, they value social connection, and seek to advance and improve their environment. The Y Generation are more comfortable with multiculturalism and use the latest electronics and Internet networking sites.

3.3 Baby busters

The baby busters, born between 1965 and 1978, are known as "Generation X." In contrast to the baby boomers before them, baby busters experienced broken families and received limited parental supervision. Many were raised in an environment with a greater diversity of lifestyles. The changing roles of men and women mean that busters are more accustomed to being on their own and are less influenced by traditional roles or authority figures.

Because of the diversity of situations in which the baby busters have been raised, they share few common traits as a group; they show strong individualistic attitudes and a cynicism about their heritage, but tend to be pragmatic about their personal and economic situations.

Having been raised with VCRs and video games, the busters are accustomed to a highly visual world. They read periodicals that have short, concise articles. The busters have few heroes, attach less importance to the establishment, are not as concerned about brand value symbols, and crave entertainment.

The busters are selective about what they buy and are less concerned with conspicuous consumption. They are more likely to buy affordable quality and meaningful products and put less emphasis on the prestige value of the product.

Communication with busters needs to be quick and to the point. Radio, for example, is highly segmented and provides program variety that suits the busters' diverse characteristics.

3.4 Seniors

The boomers' market size has for many years dominated the market. At present, 11 percent of the population is over the age of 65 and has 50 percent of the nation's discretionary income. The 65-plus market represents a gold mine for companies that can target their marketing programs to seniors.

Most of today's seniors are well educated, healthy, and active. With the seniors' stable financial position and high discretionary income, they are a ready market for a savvy company. However, do not make the mistake of treating the seniors market as homogeneous.

Over the years, seniors have had a chance to develop their own individual characteristics and may be even more diverse than younger people.

Adult consumers go through different consumer stages. Generally speaking, young adults' main concern is to acquire. Getting a car, buying clothes, and acquiring furniture for their first home consumes most of their dollars. As a rule, young adults seek products that provide self-gratification and are consistent with their image. By mid-life, people's purchases are more consistent with their identity and most buy a mix of products and services that provide a catered experience. Typically, one may upgrade an old car to a luxury model, buy good wine for dinner, and stay in a nice resort for a weekend away from home. As people get older, they go from acquiring products to seeking catered experiences.

When communicating the benefit of your product to seniors, focus on age-related concerns rather than age itself. For example, if you are selling food to seniors, focus on the fact that your product is easily digestible and soft rather than saying it is food for denture-wearers or the elderly. When positioning products for seniors, your product needs to be presented as something to be appreciated. Products for an older market should have the following characteristics:

(a) *Convenient:* Make the product easy to use, like remote controls for the radio or lights, and snap-ons and Velcro tabs instead of buttons.

(b) *Security-oriented:* There are opportunities for products that provide protection and safety. For example, deadbolt locks for doors, and absorbent products for people with bladder control problems.

(c) *Comfortable:* Products that make you feel good, like clothing that breathes well, car seats that are easy to get into and out of, and large type on menus.

(d) *Independence-oriented:* Products that free seniors from day-to-day dependence on others, like controls that are easy to reach and operate, and shovels with a smaller scoop.

4. Economy

The economic environment represents the purchasing power of consumers. It is made up of current household incomes, the price of goods, types of savings, and credit availability. In the 1970s, overall income growth after tax was more than 20 percent. Beginning in the 1980s and continuing through the 2000s, overall income growth was negligible after accounting for inflation and increased taxes. The picture provided by looking at the overall income is different when looking at income distribution.

In 1965, 25 percent of the women in Canada worked outside the home compared to 60 percent in the 1990s. In 1989, 81 percent of households earning more than $70,000 were couples, compared with 33 percent in 1967. There is a larger number of couples with similar occupations than there were in the 1960s. The end result is that income distribution among the population is highly skewed. Although there was a negligible overall increase in income compared to the 1970s, there is now a greater number of upper- and lower- income earners and fewer middle-income earners.

The recession in the early 1990s, with its high unemployment and decrease in the number of middle-income earners, hurt many major department store sales. Meanwhile, some discount stores that catered to lower-income earners did well. Also, because of an increased number of upper-income earners, sales for designer furniture, entertainment, restaurants, and fine wines increased.

A century ago, economist Ernest Engel observed that as people's earnings increase, the percentage of income spent on food, housing, and household operation remains constant while the percentage spent on clothing, health, education, and transportation increases. Engel's principle still applies in many cases today. The shift in income distribution influences the type of product and the price you can charge. Although recessions and unemployment have a large influence on the overall economies, opportunities and threats are equally presented by trends in annual income and its distribution.

5. Politics

The political environment is composed of laws, government policies, and pressure groups that can affect your business. Government can affect trade negotiation and protection, antitrust action, deregulation of industry, and the level of privatization. Government legislation has been instituted to define and prevent unfair competition, to protect consumers from disreputable business practices such as deceptive offers and bait pricing, and to protect the interests of society. This would cover such issues as contamination of air and water, and unsafe food processing procedures.

Governments are becoming more active in business policy and strategy. The formation of major trade blocs such as Unified Europe, the Asian Pacific Tariff Union, and the North American Free Trade Agreement (NAFTA) brings both opportunities and threats to your business. Deregulation had a profound effect on the airline industries in North America. The introduction of economic regulatory reform (deregulation) to encourage a more free-market orientation for airlines had a heavy impact on the industry. The reformed market resulted in a change of equipment, as well as acquisitions and mergers by the airlines, along with bankruptcies.

Interest groups, government actions, and new legislation can have profound effects on the operation of your business. As a marketer, you need a good working knowledge of the major laws and regulations that are relevant to your business.

Although some regulations may increase consumer costs and hurt legitimate business and new investment, you can save money by first being aware of the regulations that affect your business.

Businesses can do little to change the five major environmental forces of marketing. As a marketer, you need to monitor the changes that may affect your business and adapt your marketing strategy to take advantage of opportunities and avoid threats.

4
SEGMENTING YOUR MARKET AND IDENTIFYING CONSUMER BEHAVIOR

Until recently, it was standard practice for many businesses to mass-produce their product, then glut the market and advertise. As competition intensified, profit levels declined.

When firms recognized that they could not be everything to everyone, the concept of subdividing the market into submarkets or target markets became popular. For example, restaurants need to specialize their services: Some people want just a hamburger while others would like a European meal. Within the European menu, some would prefer French cuisine, others Greek dishes. The French cuisine can be further divided into those who prefer traditional French cooking and others who prefer nouvelle cuisine. Few restaurants can prepare all types of dishes and maintain a quality level attractive to customers, so each must tailor their services to a segment of the market's interests.

1. Segmentation

The objective of segmentation is to structure your products and your firm to be responsive to the submarket's needs. The different sections in a magazine are a good analogy for market segmentation. For example, *Time* magazine has sections on business, science, law, medicine, world news, and theater. By combining similar stories into sections, the reader can focus on articles of particular interest to him or her. Likewise, segmentation helps your business identify potential customers more effectively.

It is important to recognize that not all people need the same things. Single people tend to spend their money on easy-to-prepare foods, restaurant meals, dry cleaning, and entertainment. Compare that profile with a newly married couple who are setting up a home.

The couple will be likely to spend money on furniture, major appliances, and dishes. When children arrive, the couple's needs will be different again; funds will likely be channeled into baby furniture, clothing, medicine, and later into music lessons, sports equipment, and life insurance.

You must be sensitive to people's changing needs, attitudes, and values and recognize that there are groups or segments of people within a market who will benefit more from your products than others. A businessperson with limited resources cannot hope to satisfy everyone's needs.

Your potential customers within any market need to be divided into segments. There are many ways to do this. You could divide your market by geographical area, age, family size, or occupation. You could also divide your market according to social class, preferred lifestyle, or the different benefits that various groups of customers seek from your product.

For example, if you sell clothing, you might segment your market according to age. Suppose you own a retail clothing store located near a high school and there is heavy student traffic in front of your store. You have limited resources and must decide on a specific line. Given the age group that is most likely to frequent your store, you might be quite successful selling sweatshirts and jeans to appeal to teenagers and young adults.

Whichever criteria you use to segment your market, your use depends on whether you are a manufacturer, wholesaler, or retailer; the type of product you sell; how well known your product is; what the competition is doing; and your marketing needs. Segmenting is more of an art than a science. You may have to try several combinations before you gain insight into the characteristics and behaviors of your segment.

2. Segmenting Using Demographics and Psychographics

Market segmentation is the process by which you divide the market into groups of consumers who have similar needs. These groups tend to respond in similar ways to product features and functions.

You can divide your market into different groups or segments by describing each group in terms of geographic, demographic, and psychographic variables. Table 1 provides some of the segmentation variables most commonly used to segment your market.

When selecting a segmenting variable to describe your market group, it is important to remember that no single variable can fully describe your target group. Your segmentation approach is more effective when you use several segmenting variables to describe your target market.

2.1 Benefits segmentation

One of the common approaches is to determine which benefits people seek when consuming a product, who seeks these benefits, and which brand they prefer. A classic example of benefits segmentation comes from researcher Russell Haley's study on the toothpaste market. Haley identified four major segments of toothpaste users: low price, decay prevention, bright teeth, and good taste. Each group had particular characteristics that identified what they look for from toothpaste and who they are.

Low price users were mainly men who look for the cheapest brand. This segment was compiled of heavy users who are likely to buy only sale items.

TABLE 1
SEGMENTATION

GEOGRAPHICS

Region	Maritime, Eastern, South Eastern, Southern, Central, South Pacific, North Pacific
City size	Under 5,000; 5,000–20,000; 20,000–50,000; 50,000–100,000; 100,000–250,000; 250,000–500,000; 500,000–1,000,000; above 1,000,000
Density	Urban, suburban, rural
Prevailing weather	Hot, cold, temperate, dry, rainy

DEMOGRAPHICS

Age	Under 6, 7–12, 13–19, 20–24, 25–34, 35–44, 45–54, 55–64, 65+
Gender	Male, female
Income	Under $10,000, $10,000–$14,999, $15,000–$19,999, $20,000–$24,999, $25,000–$29,999, $30,000–$39,999, $40,000–$49,999, $50,000–$59,999, $60,000+, $80,000+, $100,000+
Education	Elementary school, secondary school, secondary school graduate, some community college, community college graduate, some university, university graduate, post-university degree
Occupation	Managerial, professional, technical, administrative, clerical, sales, retail, tradespersons, general labor, students, homemakers, retired, unemployed
Family size	1, 2, 3–4, 5+

HOUSEHOLD

Composition	Young and single; young, married with no children; young, married with preschoolers; young, married with child over 6; older, married with children; older, married with no children; older, married with teenagers; single
Religion	Catholic, Protestant, Buddhist, Hindu, Jew, Muslim, no affiliation
Race	Caucasian, African-American, Oriental
Nationality	American, Canadian, British, French, German, Italian, Chinese, Middle Eastern

PSYCHOGRAPHICS

Social strata	Upper class, nouveau rich, middle class, lower class
Lifestyle	Conservative, swinger, active, couch potato, achiever, wannabes, sophisticate, modest
Attitudes	Optimistic, pessimistic, impartial
Innovative	Innovator, early adopter, early majority, late majority, last-to-buy

TABLE 1 — CONTINUED

PURCHASE BEHAVIOR

Benefits	Quality, value, economy, prestige, service, convenience
Usage rate	Nonuser, light user, medium user, heavy user

TYPE OF USER

Occasional, regular

Decay prevention users were conservative and usually from large families. They were likely to buy brands they perceived to prevent tooth decay. Advertising should show positive check-ups from using the product. Another possibility is to show the approval it receives from dentists or laboratory tests.

Bright teeth users were highly sociable and active teenagers who sought toothpaste that would give them bright, white teeth. A likely advertising appeal would show people in social settings.

Good taste users were children concerned with the flavor of the toothpaste. Colorful packaging could be an appropriate appeal for this group.

Benefits segmentation seeks to identify consumer needs and provide the product they want. By understanding what the consumer wants and who they are, you can focus your marketing strategy to appeal to what your customer seeks. Although toothpaste users may want all the benefits of low price, decay prevention, bright teeth, and good taste, their attention will be drawn to the product that puts priority on what is most important to them.

In practice, business people can do much to segment their market by paying attention to their day-to-day experiences, observations, and secondary data (e.g., trade journals and discussions with customers).

For example, a manager of a building supply store wants to divide his customers into different user groups, such as commercial contractors and residential buyers. Commercial contractors want to buy in bulk at a discounted price with easy access to the yard where they can load supplies and drive away. The residential buyer is likely to ask numerous questions on what to buy and what to use.

Although you are pretty clear about what the commercial contractor wants, you notice that there is a wider range in what residential buyers want. After a discussion with a sample of customers or focus group discussions to learn what benefits they seek, when they buy, how often they use the product, how they perceive your product and service, and a small description of who they are, you can segment that market further.

After much discussion, you notice that the residential buyers can be divided into two groups: the weekend handyman and the do-it-yourselfer. You should now describe each group in terms of who they are and what major benefits they want. Your notes may tell you that the weekend handyman wants a wide selection of readily available materials. The do-it-yourselfer wants someone to explain the how-to of the job. At this stage, try to rank each group in terms of sales volume.

Having divided your market, you now have to decide who to serve and how to position yourself against your competitors. Depending on the product you carry, your finances, and staff, you may decide to cater only to commercial contractors or to residential buyers. A good understanding of the needs of each group allows you to decide what to provide and how to provide it. Like the toothpaste user, your appeal, service, and what products you provide need to be different for different groups. Once that has been determined, you can be more competitive.

2.2 Gender

Although there are obvious opportunities for gender segmentation on products such as clothing, cosmetics, and reading material, there are equal opportunities to use different appeals for men and women. An increasing number of women are buying cars, financial packages, or insurance. For example, in buying cars, women are more concerned with reliability and service. Your appeal should take this into consideration. Equally important is to provide a positive attitude that is consistent with male and female customer expectations.

Except for big ticket items such as cars and furniture, women are still making most of the household purchases, including men's personal items. However, more men are shopping, representing a market opportunity for certain types of products and appropriate appeals.

Businesses that are accustomed mainly to female consumers need to adapt to men's increasing involvement in the marketplace. Like women, men can be divided into different groups of shoppers. Some men like shopping and take time to look around for the most suitable product. Others shop only at discount stores or look for sales, while still others resist shopping until desperation sets in. However, in some areas, men's purchasing behavior differs from that of women.

One peculiarity about men is their need to know how the product works. This "need to know how it works" attitude also applies to men's choice of reading material. For example, men read magazines that discuss sports and news, as well as other "how-to" magazines.

Men also spend more time reading newspapers, but read little on home and family issues. Men like watching action-oriented programs such as sports, adventure, and science fiction on television. Like women, men like to watch documentaries, news programs, and entertainment specials. When communicating with men, advertising should be in action-oriented media.

There are opportunities for companies that can provide appropriate products and present them in a way that appeals to either men or women.

2.3 Other variables

Many other segmenting variables such as social class, lifestyle, and usage rate can be used as a basis for segmenting your market. Children of different ages are attracted to different toys. Although age is an important segmenting variable in the toy industry, age, like other segmenting variables, needs to be combined with other factors to give a more accurate picture of your target market needs.

For example, the seniors market is far from a homogeneous group; you would be mistaken to group them solely by factors of age or health. Dividing seniors into groups is more effective if you combine several segmenting variables: consumption patterns, health, sociability, age, willingness to adapt to new things, income, education, and independence.

Educational cruises and custom-made clothing, for instance, may be of interest to seniors who are independent, healthy, have sufficient income, and like to try new things.

Another more conservative, introverted group with a moderate income may be interested in gardening and landscaping products. Different groups of seniors seek very different products. Your promotional appeal will vary depending which group you choose to serve.

3. Market Positioning

Having determined which segments exist, you must decide which segment to serve and how to position your product to distinguish it from the competition.

The purpose of positioning is to establish a distinctive image that identifies your business in customers' minds. Once you have established who to serve, you must decide how best to compete within that segment. In each market segment, there will be firms offering similar benefits competing for the customer's attention. By focusing your position, you can offer something that is noticeably different.

Positioning should be based on your internal operations and your ability to provide benefits that are distinct from your competitors. For example, light beer companies position themselves among other beer companies by providing a beer low in calories. A small retail store could position itself by providing a high-quality paper bag to give the impression of quality service or, alternatively, by using newspaper wrappings to give the impression that costs are being kept down.

As you proceed to positioning, answer these questions:

- How does your customer now perceive you?

- How would you like to be perceived by your customer?

- How is the competition's position perceived?

- Are you honestly offering something different, and is it consistent with your company's goals?

- Do you have the resources to communicate your desired position with your customers? Will your customer believe your claim?

4. Understanding Customer Buying Behavior

You have identified your customer. Now you must answer the questions: What influences your customer? Why does a customer select a particular product? How can you predict which product the customer will buy?

Customer attitudes, intentions, needs, emotions, self-image, moods, and values all exert major influences on their choice of product. When customers buy a product, they go through certain stages before making a decision.

First, there is a recognition of need. What occurs to initiate a need? When does a customer say, "I want something"?

Second, there is an information search. Where does the customer look for information?

Third is the evaluation of alternatives. In evaluating different choices, which criteria do your customers use?

The fourth stage is the actual choice. What determines the selection among the alternatives?

Finally, there are the feelings the customer has after the purchase is made. "Did I make the right decision?"

At each stage, several factors affect the customer's choice. You need to identify which are the most important and exert the greatest influence on the customer's choice.

4.1 Recognition of need

The first step in the buying process occurs when an individual recognizes a need for a particular product. The need may be triggered from within as with hunger, thirst, or a desire to socialize. Or the cues may be external, such as a magazine advertisement for mocha cake that prompts him or her to go to a favorite bakery.

As a marketer, you must be able to recognize the cues that trigger interest in your product. Does the need for your product fluctuate, and should the cues differ with time? For example, in the first warm days of spring, gardeners' thoughts turn to the outdoors. This is a prime time for nurseries and garden centers to advertise. Research should establish what cues activate interest in your product.

4.2 Information search

Once a need has been recognized, a customer searches for information on how to satisfy that need. For routine purchases such as gasoline, groceries, and other items, customers don't spend much time searching; they make a decision based on habits, beliefs, and attitudes. However, if customers are unaware of different brands or types of products, they seek information from family, friends, colleagues, advertising, salespeople, displays, and brochures. For example, a study showed the following sources for choosing clothing, in order of priority: personal preferences, friends, advertising, store displays, salespeople, and fashion shows.

For routine purchases, your task as a marketer is to break the customer's habits by providing cues to call attention to your product. The cues may include point-of-purchase displays, special features, price reductions, and coupons. For more complex purchases, you must determine how and where the buyer gets the information and the importance of each source. Once you have determined what influences exist, you can more easily decide which is the best way to reach your customer.

4.3 Evaluating the alternatives

Next, the customer needs to process the information gathered to arrive at a decision. People's motivations, perceptions, learning patterns, and beliefs have an impact on the number of alternatives or attributes considered. For example, a person with a high need for security may put more importance on a product that has been recommended or endorsed by reputable, independent authorities; a person with health concerns is more likely to choose a toothpaste that prevents tooth decay than one that simply freshens breath.

Similarly, factors such as social group, family, lifestyle, and occupation also influence customers' evaluations of alternatives. A highly social person is more likely to choose a toothpaste known to brighten teeth. A family-oriented person is more likely to consider a station wagon or van than a sports car.

Information on which factors influence the customer's judgment and which attributes of the product convey those impressions can be very valuable. Based on this information, you can decide which attributes to emphasize in the advertising campaign, whether to introduce a new product that is closer to the ideal brand, whether to modify the existing packaging and product features to come closer to the attributes preferred by the desired segment, whether to call attention to attributes customers are not aware of, or whether to correct misconceptions about the product's attributes.

4.4 Choice

After evaluating the alternatives, the customer lists his or her choices in order of priorities. Under normal conditions, the customer picks the option he or she prefers most, but other factors can intervene.

An individual may postpone his or her decision to buy because of perceived risks. There are five major types of risk a customer may consider:

(a) Financial (Can I afford it? Do I get value for my money?)

(b) Performance (Will the product work?)

(c) Physical (Is there potential harm to me as the user?)

(d) Psychological (Is it consistent with my self-image?)

(e) Social (Is it accepted by others?)

Other factors such as an expected increase or decrease in salary, a salesperson's mannerism, or office surroundings may also deter the buyer from making the preferred choice.

To reduce risks, customers either buy endorsed, familiar, and guaranteed products, or avoid making the decision. The marketer must detect which are the predominant risks and provide information to reduce those risks. Additional inducements at this stage can help alleviate anxiety.

4.5 Post-purchase feelings

Based on the customer's expectations and the product's perceived performance, customers experience either satisfaction or dissatisfaction after buying a product. The marketer should try to obtain honest information from the customer after his or her purchase. This can be done by means of a questionnaire, warranty reply, or after-sale phone survey.

Dissatisfaction can produce poor public relations. If the customer is dissatisfied, it may be that your claim is not consistent with customers' perceptions. Action should be taken to either portray the product in a more realistic way or modify the product. You can also reduce dissatisfaction by providing additional information or assistance after the purchase has been made.

Complete the following questions; they are designed to help you segment your market and analyze how customers view your product.

QUESTIONS

MARKET SEGMENTATION

1. What possible new services or products could be developed for existing or potential customers?

_____

_____

_____

_____

_____

2. Who is your target market? Describe people in your market (e.g., gender, age group, profession).

_____

_____

_____

_____

_____

3. What benefit is your market seeking from your product? Do different groups seek different benefits? Describe each group.

_____

_____

_____

_____

_____

4. Is there one group of customers that uses your product more extensively than the others? Describe them.

_____

_____

_____

_____

_____

5. Describe your product from the customer's point of view.

_____

_____

_____

_____

_____

5
RESEARCHING YOUR MARKET

1. Areas to Research

1.1 Who is your market?

You must consider the age of your market, whether the individuals are married or single, their gender, whether they are trend conscious, what their population growth rate is, whether there are legal or political constraints, and if there are technological changes that could make your product obsolete.

1.2 What products do they buy?

It is easy to assume that everyone will like your product as much as you do. However, your banker or investor wants to know what your market is looking for: a convenience item, impulse item, or luxury item. What benefits does your product offer? How is it different from the competition?

1.3 When do they buy?

What time of the day or year does your customer buy? Do people buy only during economic upswings? Do they need your product on an ongoing basis? If so, you need to constantly remind your customers about your products.

1.4 Who is involved in the purchase decision?

Who initiates the buying process? Who gathers the information? Who makes the decision to buy? Do buyers get their information about your product from friends, television, radio, or other advertising? Do peer groups, colleagues, and neighbors influence the buyer's decision? By considering all the players involved, you may begin to realize how important research is to target accurately.

1.5 Where is your market?

Is your market national, regional, or local? Which media best reaches your customers?

1.6 Where should you sell your product?

Should you sell your product through catalogues, mail order, department stores, or specialty shops?

1.7 Why does the market buy your product?

Is your product purchased to satisfy a safety need, a need for status, a spiritual need? What features of your product best meet those needs?

There are various marketing research methods that you can use to provide you with all the answers to these questions. However, before you decide to conduct research, check to see if the information is already available.

2. Secondary Data

Secondary data are research materials that have already been collected and published. You should always start researching with secondary data, which are inexpensive, quick to obtain, and can provide valuable guidance.

The following sources of secondary data can help you define areas where additional information is required or where problems may arise. With the information available, it may be possible to solve the problems without additional expense. Should more information be required, you must then consider the next step, which is formal research, to collect what is known as primary data (see section **3.** below).

2.1 Government

The federal government furnishes more marketing data than any other source in the country. In addition, check regional government sources. Most departments also publish special research issues in their field of expertise. Look in the telephone book or on the Internet for government listings and start your inquiries.

2.2 Trade, professional, and business associations

Trade journals and periodic reports can be excellent sources of information in their areas.

2.3 College, university, and research organizations

The range of business research issued is wide and can be invaluable. Most post-secondary institutions have specialized research departments.

2.4 Libraries

Good libraries have books, newspapers, and magazines on various industries. Also consider scholarly journals, such as *Journal of Consumer Research, Journal of Marketing,* and periodicals such as *Advertising Age, Business Periodical Index,* and *Fortune.*

2.5 Marketing firms

Advertising agencies, sales management firms, marketing research firms, and many magazine, radio, television, and newspaper companies may all have marketing data and old studies that can be of value to your business.

2.6 Consultants

Private consultants are available; check the Yellow Pages. In the United States, the federal government sponsors a consulting assistance program through the Small Business Administration (SBA) as well as the Service Corps of Retired Executives program (SCORE). In Canada, contact the Business Development Bank of Canada (BDC) and inquire about the Counselling Assistance to Small Enterprises program (CASE). Also ask at regional small business advisory departments.

3. Primary Data

Primary data are used when secondary data do not exist or the information available is unsuitable. Collect the information yourself or hire professional assistance.

The decision to hire professional help depends on the type and extent of the research, the value of your investment, the time you have available, and your financial resources. Many marketing research firms are available to provide you with the help you may need. The marketplace is very competitive, so make sure you receive comparative cost estimates. Ask for references and check them out.

Research can provide crucial information for making decisions, but it can be both expensive and time consuming. The cost of research must be balanced against potential losses due to a poor decision based on insufficient information. If the risk is small or the product inexpensive to produce, you may decide to go ahead. However, if the risk is moderate to high or the product is expensive to produce, you may want guidance before making major decisions based on your research.

There are many ways you can carry out your own research. The following is a brief description of the major marketing research methods.

3.1 Sales records

Sales records are a valuable source of information and can be broken down in a variety of ways, such as by territory, salesperson, or customer. You also need to keep track of the cost of sales as well as the timing of your advertising run, sales promotions, and changes in prices or product lines.

Keeping good records allows you to compare, for example, pre- and post-promotion sales to determine how many new customers you gained through a promotion. Based on the cost of the promotion, you can decide if it's worth repeating. Good records show if sales discounts or extra service provide extra sales. Measure the additional cost against the extra sales to see what level of service you can provide without jeopardizing your profit.

When looking at your sales record for information, remember that many other factors may influence your sales volume changes. However, under most circumstances, your sales record and analysis can provide valuable guidance in your marketing decision.

3.2 Order-billing-shipping account

The order-billing-shipping account system will tell you how long it takes to service a customer. How does this compare with the competition? Customer accounts, warranty claims, and returns should also be recorded. This allows you to determine if servicing certain customer categories costs more than others. On the warranty or return card, if you ask for customer information such as occupation, category, age, family size, and income, you can watch for emerging trends.

3.3 Sales representatives

Your best source of external information is your own sales force. They can provide you with valuable, inexpensive, and readily available information about the marketplace. They can tell you if a certain shirt color is not selling anymore or if your merchandise is being placed on the bottom shelf by retailers. Research has shown that between 60 to 85 percent of product improvements come from paying attention to customers' comments.

If you want to maximize the information obtained from your employees, you have to encourage listening and, if necessary, teach them how to listen to customers and seek their opinions. You will be amazed at how much you and your staff can learn from people this way.

3.4 Questionnaires

A questionnaire provides a standardized format for asking questions and makes analyzing the results easier. Multiple choice or yes/no questionnaires are well-suited to gathering information on desired product features, media effectiveness (tracking), sales promotion effectiveness, preferred services, and favored distribution systems.

Before preparing a questionnaire, consult a book on questionnaire design; there are many dos and don'ts. Your choice of words, the type and sequence of questions, and the available answers all influence the quality of your research. Your questionnaire should be simple and ask only pertinent questions.

Equally important is the sample size and choice. The sample design determines how many people are interviewed, who is interviewed, and how they are selected. Results from a poor sample are not going to help you.

The questionnaire can either be used by an interviewer at a shopping mall, on a street corner, or in your store, or it can be mailed to a select group of people. Sometimes you may have to provide incentives such as coupons, free samples, or gift certificates to entice people to respond to your questionnaire.

3.5 Group survey

Compared to questionnaires, a survey is a relatively unstructured interview. Typically, 6 to 12 people gather for a few hours to discuss your product, its price, and your company's services. A team leader asks questions and encourages the group to discuss different aspects of your product. The leader tape records the session for further analysis. Because of the unstructured questions and open comments, surveys are often difficult to compare. However, group surveys are particularly useful for exploratory research and can provide a broad range of information on customers' opinions, feelings, and motives.

3.6 Telephone survey

Telephone surveys can be used to conduct either a structured questionnaire-type interview or an unstructured interview. The telephone survey is a very quick and inexpensive way to gather information. It is particularly suited for well-known products and established businesses.

3.7 Expert opinions

You can gather valuable information about your product by speaking with various professionals. For example, suppose you have just invented a new exercise hand weight. You could ask aerobics instructors, sports medicine doctors, physiotherapists, athletes, bodybuilders, and athletic trainers for their opinions on your product's usefulness, appearance, desirability, and design.

3.8 Mail-order catalog

To get a feeling for the demand of your product, you may wish to send a sample or a picture to several mail-order houses. These houses employ professionals to select from among potential products those that have a good chance of making a profit. If you receive several positive letters about your product, you may have a winner.

3.9 Test market

A test market can be very useful to many small businesses that want to try their product before launching it on the market. For example, let's suppose you have invented a child's toy or game. Here are some simple and inexpensive tests that could help you determine the toy's potential.

(a) Buy several toys that are similar to your prototype. Leave your toy with the others on the floor of your house and invite five to ten couples with children. Observe if the children play with your toy, how they use it, and for how long. Ask them what they like about your toy and which toy they like the most.

(b) Go to several stores and look at competing toys and consider their price, how they work, how they are packaged and promoted, who the market is, how your idea differs, and how your toy compares.

(c) Call a department store, get a buyer's name, make an appointment, and give a brief presentation. Buyers see hundreds of different toys. They can give you valuable advice about packaging, promotion, pricing, modifications, and market potential.

(d) Once you are satisfied you have a competitive product, run in-store tests. Ask buyers to put the toy on their shelves for a while. In return, you will likely have to provide a box of toys at no charge to the store or some other incentive.

   From the retailer you want to know if the toy sells, if the price is acceptable to customers, if they like the packaging, and if customers and store employees have suggestions about improvements. Ask for honest and objective opinions.

(e) If you have more resources, you may want to test the market in two or three different cities or separate locations within the same city using different price levels, packaging, and promotions. Ask the same questions as you did with the first test market. Compare results of different sites to help you determine which is the most favorable marketing mix.

Note: If your product or idea is easily duplicated, you may have to stay away from test marketing. Competitors can quickly duplicate your idea and beat you to the marketplace. If your product is not available, a model or prototype could be substituted. For best results, your model should look as close as possible to the finished product.

3.10 Trade shows

Trade shows combine some of the advantages of the "test market" and "expert opinion" research techniques. For a small price, you can rent a booth and show your product to both potential buyers and professionals.

3.11 Direct mail

Direct mail can be a valuable research tool to check out different advertising appeals, product features, and prices. For example, three different message appeals could be sent to three different groups of people.

By indicating on the return coupon which message was used, you can monitor which brought the highest percentage return. Likewise, different price and product features could be tested. See Appendix 1 for more about researching your market and making forecasts.

6
DEVELOPING YOUR PRODUCT

The most basic marketing question your business faces is "What product do we provide to our target market?" The product should appeal to and be consistent with the needs, values, and lifestyles of your target market. In the conceptualization of your product, you should consider the following.

1. What Benefits Are You Offering?

A successful product must benefit your customers. The most fundamental questions you must answer are —

(a) What do my customers really need?

(b) What are my customers' perceived needs?

(c) Am I satisfying those needs?

For example, clothing provides more than protection from the weather; it also says something about the wearer and the people he or she associates with on a social or business level. A sofa is not just a piece of furniture; it provides comfort as well as clues about the person's lifestyle.

2. How Do You Convey the Benefits of a Product?

Customers must believe your product can provide the benefits you claim. Customers judge the value of your product by the following means.

2.1 Interest value

Interest value is the pleasure derived from using the product or the reward gained from having the product. Yogurt, chocolate, or television can fill hunger and entertainment needs, but are also rewards for a hard day's work or the ingredients of a special evening.

2.2 Identity

A customer's choice of products says something about his or her personality and lifestyle. For example, a silk dress, a brass lamp, a brand of perfume, or a bottle of champagne all convey a certain style and character.

2.3 Risk

Consumers are also concerned about the possibility and importance of a bad purchase. For example, when someone buys a washing machine, vacuum cleaner, mattress, or car battery, he or she runs the risk of making the wrong selection. A customer wants a battery that works in an emergency, a mattress that does not cause back pain, and a vacuum cleaner that does what it says it will do. Guarantees and warranties are ways of reducing the risk factor.

2.4 Packaging

Years ago, packaging was a minor part of marketing; today it is important and serves many purposes. It protects goods from breaking, shrinking, and spoiling. It reduces the cost of transportation of the goods. It can create the impression of a "new product" by changing the shape or quantity of the goods. It can be a valuable promotional tool by attracting attention and describing the product, and it can attract your target market by using appealing colors, styles, shapes, and textures. By adding your brand name to the goods, it can generate further advertising.

2.5 Branding

Branding refers to the use of a name, symbol, or design to identify your goods from those of your competitors. Research shows that customers feel safer buying an endorsed, familiar, or well-known brand. Here are some advantages to branding:

- It helps customers identify your product and makes shopping for it easier.

- It protects your product features from imitation.

- Certain brands are associated with quality and others with status which appeal to customers who desire these psychological and symbolic values (e.g., Mercedes, BMW).

- It encourages repeat purchases if the company consistently maintains its service and quality.

- It helps build a corporate image.

- It may develop customer allegiance by becoming a "household word" (e.g., Xerox, Band-Aid, and Aspirin).

A good brand name can help communicate something about your product and the service you provide. When you select a brand name, observe the following rules:

- It should be easy to pronounce and read.

- It should be easy to recognize and remember.

- It should say something about your product.

- It shouldn't be offensive or negative.

- It should be able to last through time.

- It should be distinct.

- It should be short and simple.

2.6 Customer contact

Customers often judge your product by your sales and service rather than by the product itself. The competence, experience, personality, and communication skills of your personnel must be pleasing to them.

Similarly, remember that customers are influenced by the type and style of your facilities, the ease of access to your location, and your hours of operation.

2.7 Service availability

The time the customer has to wait to receive the product and the time it takes to perform a service can influence the perception of the quality of your product. People dislike waiting. On the other hand, when customers are being served, they like to feel they are receiving your full attention without interruptions. Your schedule needs to balance both the time you give to your customer and the time he or she has to wait to receive service.

2.8 Green marketing

The first wave of "green marketing" occurred in the late 1980s and early 1990s. Greater public attention to environmental issues occurred in the early 2000s when Al Gore spoke about the environment. Continuing discussion with the European Commission, the United States, and China on how best to cut carbon emissions will bring increasing demand for energy-efficient products. Rising energy prices, pollution concerns, and water shortages will, in future, create business opportunities for products marketed as "green."

From hybrid cars that use less fuel to non-toxic paint, your product, if possible, should use less energy and be non-polluting. Producing smaller water heaters, more efficient washing machines, insulation for hot water pipes, and thermal-resistant skylight glazing, are all examples of products considered good for the environment.

There is no consensus by consumers, entrepreneurs, and activists on what constitutes green marketing, but it is gaining momentum in importance. Green marketing, as defined by the American Marketing Association, is the marketing of products that are presumed to be environmentally safe. Thus green marketing includes a broad range of activities related not only to the properties of your product, but also the production process; the packaging you use; as well as your organization's management, operational practices, and usage of communication systems.

With growing attention on the reduction of carbon emissions, more and more consumers will demand a green approach. Going green may bring you greater profit as well as curtail criticism.

Although a great number of people express concern over the environment, the vast majority of consumers will ask, "What's in it for me?" In order to be successful at green marketing you must satisfy your customer's needs while in some way making your product good for the environment. Many customers are not willing to pay an extra premium despite their proclaimed concern for the environment. In addition to being good for the environment, your product must offer desirable benefits. If buying green products requires sacrifice, few customers will buy your product. Your product must be superior in performance, provide convenience, be healthy and safe, and provide greater efficiency. To be safe from criticism, your green claim should be pulled from secondary sources, and specific to the benefits provided by your product.

Before you embark on green marketing, be aware that customers are sometimes skeptical of green claims. Your reputation can be seriously damaged if your green claim is discovered to be false or inconsistent with your other products, related services, or operational practices. Hardly a week goes by without a large company announcing that it just reduced its carbon footprint by installing a new videoconference room, or switched its car fleet to hybrid cars. So it is not just your product that must be green, but also your practices and operations.

There are many ways you can make business greener. Before purchasing goods or services, consider how green the product or service is compared to other products on the market. In doing so, you must consider the entire product life cycle from manufacturing, transportation, retailing, and disposal. There is much energy and cost efficiency in making your business environmentally friendly. Consider the following options:

- Turn off your equipment and computer at the end of the day.

- Encourage communication by email, and print only if necessary.

- Print double-sided (rather than single-sided) documents.

- Before purchasing any new product, see if you can refurbish an existing one.

- Turn your thermostat down.

There are many more ways you can save on cost and energy and be environmentally friendly. You must put into practice what you say, and your product as well as your practices must be consistent.

When you are messaging your existing or potential customers, it is important to inform them of the steps your company is taking to demonstrate your green practices.

3. Additional Services

Additional services are those provided above and beyond what is required. For example, hotels may leave chocolates, wine, or a fluffy robe in your room. A furniture store may extend the terms of payment to regular customers.

In a competitive environment, additional services add distinction to your product and demonstrate that you care for your customers.

4. Product Life Cycle

Products go through what is commonly called a "product life cycle" which provides a useful model to evaluate the different marketing strategies that should be applied as your product goes through the different stages of its cycle. Depending on which stage your product is in, different communication appeals, pricing strategies, and promotional offers should be used.

There are four major stages in the product life cycle: Introduction, Growth, Maturity, and Decline. The time a product takes to go through each stage depends on the type of product and the new market demands created as a result of a change in technology, competition, customer taste and attitude, and the type of customer you are catering to.

In the clothing industry, changing fads and consumer tastes can turn yesterday's dream garment into tomorrow's nightmare. In the electronics industry, a technological breakthrough could bring an established, mature product to a quick decline. The disk camera is an example of a product whose quick introduction was equally matched by its quick decline. Oat bran and granola bars enjoyed a modest mature phase. Diet Coke and Swatch provide excellent examples of an extended mature phase.

The product life cycle concept requires that you take a long-term view of your marketing strategy. The shape of the product life cycle varies from industry to industry. Sample 1 represents a typical S-shape curve of the average product life cycle.

The product life cycle assumes that products have a limited life value in the marketplace and that each stage represents different opportunities and problems for distinct marketing strategies.

SAMPLE 1
AVERAGE PRODUCT LIFE CYCLE

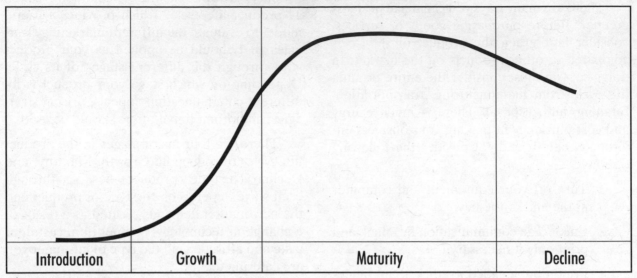

| Introduction | Growth | Maturity | Decline |

4.1 Introduction

The introduction stage is characterized by slow sales growth and negligible profits because of high production, promotional, and distribution expenses and the time required to achieve customer acceptance.

The introduction stage starts when a new product is first made available. At this stage, the company may face production and technical capability problems. For most companies, the major problems are getting adequate distribution capability and overcoming customer reluctance to change consumption patterns. Freeze-dried coffee and frozen orange juice took years before they were accepted; the market was concerned about the freshness and taste of a frozen product.

Marketing strategy for the introduction stage

Typical customer: When launching a new product, your most likely customer, known as an "innovator," is generally younger, well-educated, and cosmopolitan. The innovator is a heavy user of technical media such as trade journals and likes to be the first to use a new product.

Competition: Limited to nonexistent.

Overall strategy: Persuade the innovator to try your product.

Product: Introduce new product.

Distribution: Use selective distribution outlets.

Price: Charge a high price to recover costs when buyers are able to pay the higher price. Charge a low price when customers are price sensitive and there is strong potential for competition. The first cellular phones on the market were much more expensive than today's high-tech, lower cost models.

Promotion: Your communication should be informative and should stress the excitement of being first. Provide technical information on the benefits of your product and use media such as technical or professional journals and trade shows.

The promotion level should be high when the market is unaware of the product and low if the market is aware of the product.

4.2 Growth

If the market is satisfied with your product, sales will increase. The growth stage is characterized by a rapid climb in sales due to growing demand.

In the growth stage, competitors enter the market with new product features. The increased number of competitors and the new product variations result in an increased number of distribution outlets and market exposure. In the growth phase, a trade-off must be made between high profit margins or additional expenditures required for higher market shares.

Marketing strategy for the growth stage

Typical customer: At this stage, many of your new customers, often referred to as "early adopters," are people who are socially well-integrated within their community. They often serve as role models.

A second group, the "early majority," is slightly above average in social and economic status. As a group, they are deliberate and adopt the product just before the average. They prefer their information from reliable contacts.

Competition: Some copycats. There is an increase in the number of distribution outlets.

Overall strategy: Mass market penetration.

Product: Improved product quality, new product features.

Distribution: Seek to expand your distribution channels and outlets.

Price: High when demand is high. In the later part of the growth phase, you may consider lowering your price to attract a new layer of price-sensitive customers.

Promotion: Moderate level of promotion. Use mainly advertising to create product conviction. In the early growth stage your advertising should stress credibility, prestige, and testimonials from respected people. In the later part of the growth stage and in the early part of the maturity stage, your advertising should stress material design and its acceptability.

4.3 Maturity

The mature stage is characterized by a cut in profit margins because of intensified competition.

In the mature phase, the distribution channels are saturated and most potential customers have tried the product. The high number of competitors gives rise to overcapacity and intensified competition which leads to heavy price cuts, product modifications, and the search for new markets.

Marketing strategy for the maturity stage

Typical customer: The "late majority" is skeptical and adopts products just after the average consumer. They rely mainly on informal sources for product information.

Competition: Intense competition fighting for a piece of the pie.

Overall strategy: Defend brand position.

Product: Most products in the marketplace are in the mature stage. Sales can be revitalized by modifying your product.

Improve quality by making your product more reliable and durable. Add new features to increase convenience and safety. Change packaging to meet current styles and improve the aesthetic appearance.

Distribution: Use heavy trade allowances to retain shelf space. Enter new markets by appealing to new segments (e.g., Johnson & Johnson promoted their baby shampoo to adult users).

Attract competitors' customers. Export to foreign markets. Improve service by providing faster delivery, free wrapping, and better guarantees.

Price: Price is based on what the market will bear. You may lower your price to attract new users, but not to the point of a price war. Provide volume discounts, easier credit, and specials.

Promotion: Use advertising to differentiate your product from the competition. Expenditure levels should be modest because of high market awareness.

Show new uses. For example, baking soda used as a deodorizer in the refrigerator.

Encourage more usage from existing customers. For example, orange juice being promoted as a breakfast drink, a mixer, and a recipe ingredient.

Your appeal should highlight the quality of the design and special features of your product. Peer pressure, emotional appeal, and personal contact are effective at the maturity stage.

4.4 Decline

The decline stage is characterized by a downward shift in sales and profit erosion because of increased costs created by a decline in sales volume.

Advances in technology and shifts in consumer tastes result in a decline in total sales volume. Increased competition results in more price cutting and loss of profits. Some small profit may be gained late in the decline stage as competitors move out.

Marketing strategy for the decline stage

Typical customer: Tradition bound.

Competition: Declining as some competitors opt out.

Overall strategy: Plan for removal.

Product: Selective removal from unpromising customers while maintaining profitable niches. Complete removal of the product.

Note: Much energy can be diverted from searching for profitable replacements by thinking sales will improve when the economy picks up. Although this is possible, you need to take a hard look to see if your product matches market trends.

Distribution: Phase out unprofitable outlets.

Price: Low enough to liquidate inventory.

Promotion: Minimum expenditures and selective promotion to profitable niches.

Unfortunately, most companies do not handle the sales decline well. They retain the product hoping sales will improve. This can be expensive considering the effort and cost that goes into advertising and the time taken by sales personnel selling the product. There are also hidden costs such as poor morale and misdirected energy and priorities. As sales decline, replace the product, change it, or explore new market opportunities.

The product life cycle concept provides a means to evaluate your marketing strategy across time. In the introduction stage, your appeal to innovators with technical information is very different from the emotional appeal used in the mature stage to differentiate your product from the competition. Although in practice many products may not follow the typical product life cycle, it still remains a useful concept to plan your marketing strategy over time. The questions on the following pages can help you identify your product's life cycle.

1. What does your product do for your customer? What does it not do?

   _____
   _____
   _____
   _____
   _____
   _____
   _____

2. Could people not now using your product benefit by using it? Who are these people?

   _____
   _____
   _____
   _____
   _____
   _____
   _____

3. Can you think of any ways your product features could be improved or made safer?

   _____
   _____
   _____
   _____
   _____
   _____
   _____

4. At what stage of the life cycle is your product? (Is your product known, are competitors coming in, is competition fierce, profit margins low, sales volume declining?)

   _____
   _____
   _____
   _____
   _____
   _____

5. What choices are there available in the market in your product area?

_____
_____
_____
_____
_____
_____

6. What are the exclusive features and benefits of your product?

_____
_____
_____
_____
_____
_____

7. Does your brand name describe your product? Is it easily remembered, distinct, proven, reliable? Can people differentiate your product from its competitors?

_____
_____
_____
_____
_____
_____

8. Is your product easy to understand and use? If not, how can you help customers overcome reluctance to your product?

_____
_____
_____
_____
_____
_____
_____

7
PRICING TO SELL

Pricing is an ongoing concern. Competition from comparable products, production over-capacity, mass retailing, increased consumer price-sensitivity, competition, and aggressive penetration pricing tactics all affect pricing.

Price changes, compared to changes in product, advertising, or distribution, can be made quickly, and are often overlooked as an opportunity to boost profits. However, a quick price change does not mean guesswork pricing. Charging the right price can boost profits quickly; charging the wrong price can shrink profits just as quickly.

Pricing is an intricate issue that needs to be linked to many aspects of a business. Pricing relates to industry supply and demand, customer perception of product benefits, the competitive environment, and expected margins from different members in the distribution channels.

Traditionally, accountants and finance people used cost-plus pricing, as discussed in section **2.** below. Cost information came from a sensible accounting system made decades ago when corporate overhead could easily be allocated to a narrow range of products, direct labor costs, and materials. Today's pricing strategies need to combine hard data from an activity-based cost system with soft data from marketing.

1. What Are Your Pricing Goals?

1.1 Maximizing your profit

From an economist's point of view, profit maximization is setting a price at a level to attain the highest possible current profit. However, setting a price to maximize short-term profit, or charging what the market will bear, could diminish your chances for optimum long-term returns.

The key to profit maximization is setting a price high enough to cover your cost and earn maximum revenue, yet low enough to warrant repeat purchases, referrals, and customer loyalty.

1.2 Getting your share of the market

Your goal should be to price your product at a level that will attain a desired market share. Large companies like Sears and Standard Oil maintain a market share policy. To follow their example, you need to take a careful look at how your competition handles pricing.

If you establish your market share policy by setting your price based on the industry norm, you can be more confident that your business will do well in both good and bad economic times. Stable pricing deters price wars from developing and allows you to match your competition, which is necessary when competitive products are similar or where the market is price sensitive.

Of course your pricing policy also depends on other marketing considerations such as improving product features, services, or promotion. Your price would be lower, for instance, if you provided less service than a competing business.

1.3 Obtaining a return on your investment

You want to establish a price that will provide a certain percentage return on investment or sales. For example, some large multi-national companies have a pricing objective of a 20 percent return on investment after tax.

2. Attaining Your Pricing Goals

You want to be flexible in your pricing strategy. Pricing is influenced by circumstances that change with time, technology, competition, and promotion. Be aware of changes that directly affect your business. If there is late frost in California this year, for example, the price for your strawberries will likely go up.

Your pricing strategies should respond to changing conditions. Before setting your price, be sure to gather information on your competitors' prices and the effect your price will have on your production, inventories, costs, cash flow, and profits.

Several pricing strategies are discussed here. You can work out your own pricing policy as you work through the questions that follow this chapter.

2.1 Cost-plus pricing

The most common pricing method is known as cost-plus. The price is determined by adding a percentage for profits above the average unit cost. The average unit cost represents the total fixed cost plus the variable cost divided by the total number of items sold. The fixed cost represents the overhead expenses that don't change with the volume of work such as rent, depreciation, property taxes, insurance, maintenance, managers' salaries, and administrative expenses. The variable cost represents expenses that can change based on the volume of work such as parts, material, packaging, labor, outgoing freight, overtime pay, or commission on sales.

In practice, determining your average unit cost or determining which portion of overhead expenses are applicable to the average unit cost can be difficult. Many companies add a standard markup above a standard cost based on standard volume. For example, a retailer may add a percentage markup to the purchase cost of goods. The markup is estimated to be sufficient to cover expenses and provide a reasonable profit.

To illustrate cost-plus pricing, consider the following example: a manufacturer makes 25,000 decorative ceramic tiles. Your accounting manager provides you with the following cost breakdown for manufacturing tiles over one year.

Total variable costs	$50,000
Fixed costs	$50,000
Units sold	25,000

Unit cost = (Total variable costs + Fixed costs) ÷ Units sold

$$= (\$50,000 + \$50,000) ÷ 25,000$$

$$= \$100,000 ÷ 25,000$$

$$= \$4.00 \text{ per unit}$$

2.1.a Markup

Depending on the industry, the product, and your marketing strategy, the markup range could vary widely, and these ranges will change depending on the economic conditions.

Markup is the amount that is added to the cost to determine the selling price. Markup is expressed as a percentage of cost. Your markup percentage should be enough to cover unassigned costs and provide a reasonable profit. Let's say you want a 15 percent rate of return or markup on your merchandise. What retail price should you charge?

Selling price = Unit cost + (Unit cost x Rate of return)

$$= \$4.00 + (\$4.00 \times 15\%)$$

$$= \$4.00 + \$0.60$$

$$= \$4.60$$

The definitions for markup and margin are sometimes used differently. The standard formula for markup is:

Markup = (Unit price – Unit cost) ÷ Unit cost x 100

If you were given the above sales price and the cost, the markup would be calculated as follows:

$$= (\$4.60 – \$4.00) ÷ \$4.00 \times 100$$

$$= \$0.60 ÷ \$4.00 \times 100$$

$$= 15\%$$

2.1.b Margin

Margin is markup expressed as a percentage of price. Let's say you want to have a 15 percent profit margin. The selling price would then be:

Selling price = Unit cost ÷ (1 – Desired return on sales)

$$= \$4.00 ÷ (1 – 15\%)$$

$$= \$4.00 ÷ (1 – 0.15)$$

$$= \$4.71$$

The standard formula for margin is:

Margin = (Unit price – Unit cost) ÷ Price x 100

If you were given the above sale price and the cost, the margin would be calculated as follows:

$$= (\$4.71 – \$4.00) ÷ \$4.71 \times 100$$

$$= \$0.71 ÷ \$4.71 \times 100$$

$$= 15\%$$

The cost-plus pricing method is easier to apply in relation to other common pricing methods. However, you should remember that cost does not determine price — cost determines the different profit levels at different prices.

This approach is simple, it avoids excessive price competition, and it is often seen as "fair" by the customer. The disadvantages are that it is not responsive to market fluctuations, and you may lose customers to a competitor who uses a market share objective approach.

2.2 Target market share

A large market share provides exposure and possibly long-term security. A business that wants to increase its market share may lower its prices. Lowering your price may be advisable if —

(a) customers are price conscious,

(b) you have the production capacity or excess personnel,

(c) there is an economy of scale in production,

(d) a lower price would not be perceived as an indication of poor quality,

(e) it would discourage the competition, or

(f) a price reduction would increase market awareness.

2.3 Price skimming

Price skimming means setting a high price to maximize early cash recovery before catering to the more price sensitive segments of the market. Price skimming may be suitable if —

(a) you have a distinct and unique product and there is little competition,

(b) you are not sure what price to charge (it is easier to bring your price down than to increase it),

(c) you have limited production capacity,

(d) you appeal to a market segment that is relatively insensitive to price,

(e) it would be useful as a promotional strategy (e.g., as the product passes through its life cycle, you may lower the price to attract new markets),

(f) there is little danger of competition,

(g) the high price conveys quality, or

(h) there is little economy of scale in producing more.

2.4 Penetration pricing

Penetration pricing is comparable to a sales promotion where you substantially reduce the price on your product to retain or attract customers. The object is to have customers buy more at the full price or have your product reach the mass market immediately. Penetration pricing is possible when —

(a) customers are price sensitive,

(b) unit production costs can be reduced by producing more, and

(c) a low price would discourage the competition from entering the market.

There are two main dangers to a penetration pricing strategy. The first is that new customers who are attracted by a special offer may only purchase the product on special and not at its regular price in the future.

The second danger is that the penetration price could start a price war in which everyone would lose. This happens occasionally among gas stations or supermarkets.

2.5 Prestige pricing

Prestige pricing means charging more than the competition to sell a quality image or status product. Rolls Royce, Gucci, and Abercrombie & Fitch use this strategy.

3. Demand-Oriented Pricing

The price of a product is largely determined by how difficult it is to make and its usefulness to the customer. Price carries information about the product value and its strengths and weaknesses. The demand for your product and the price paid is what a consumer is willing to sacrifice among competing offers to acquire your product.

3.1 Price elasticity

Price elasticity is a measure of how sensitive consumers are to a price change. Price sensitivity depends on several factors. When a product is assumed to have unique qualities or values or is related to prestige or is exclusive, buyers are less sensitive to increased prices. Buyers are also less sensitive to increased prices for low-cost items when they are not aware of substitutes or when it is difficult to compare products.

Consumers may not react to a price change when there is little competition, or when buyers are slow to change their buying habits. Consumers are more willing to pay for well-known products than unknown products. Normally, the more you charge, the less you sell. However, this is not always the case. Sometimes, when you increase price, sales are unaffected.

3.2 Prices and profits

Profit is the difference between revenue and cost. It is a common belief that higher prices lead to higher profits. Although higher profit margins can lead to higher total profits, there is a trade-off between higher profit margins and sales volumes. For example, a 10 percent price increase on appliances could give you a higher profit margin but lead to a 20 percent reduction in sales volume.

In such a situation, the higher profit margin would not compensate for the lost sales volume. A 10 percent price reduction could result in a lower profit margin with a 20 percent increase in sales volume and higher total profits. This last scenario is true as long as there are no substantial costs associated with increased sales volume.

Because consumer price sensitivity varies for different products, there are situations where a price increase does not result in a substantial decrease in sales volume. In such a situation, a higher price results in a higher profit margin and higher total profits. As one can see, there is an optimal price that a business should charge. If you charge above or below the optimal price, profits will decline.

Overall, the demand for your product is largely related to how sensitive customers are to price. What price should you charge? There are three main methods to determine price demand.

3.2.a Ask the customer

Ask a sample of customers what price they are willing to pay for your product. The concept of having a fixed price is a relatively modern concept developed by F.W. Woolworth for expediency in his large-scale retailing stores.

Your product's durability, reliability, or quality of service should be clearly identified and understood before you ask what price they are willing to pay. Do not inflate or undermine the value of the products.

In the marketplace, consumer choices involve trade-offs against other offers. A second method in determining price demand is to present a sample of customers with competing products, and ask them to rate each product according to the perceived benefits they provide and ask the price they are willing to pay for each product in relation to each other.

The second method can be varied by presenting the different products at different prices. You can ask customers what they would be willing to pay if an additional service was added or if they are willing to pay extra for technological improvements, better delivery, longer guarantees, or for full service.

Alternatively, you could ask a sample of customers if they would prefer to pay less, and what part of the package they are willing to remove from the product in exchange for the lower price.

This method is particularly well-suited to existing products that you want to modify or for the introduction of new products and services.

3.2.b Ask the experts

Most retailers, wholesalers, manufacturing managers, and technical specialists have a good knowledge and understanding of their customers and the price they are willing to pay. Prepare a number of questions that relate to realistic scenarios of customer pricing issues, and ask each expert or manager how much they think customers are willing to pay under different competitive situations.

An outsider should interview at least five or more experts. Experts or managers from different backgrounds, departments, and with diverse interests should be interviewed.

This method is very useful for new products, a new competitive situation, or anywhere else it is important that the competitors don't learn of your intentions.

3.2.c Observe the market

Observe the difference in sales volumes under different prices at different times or in different areas. If you are selling wild rice, you could charge three different prices several months apart and then measure the different sales volumes. You could apply this method by also charging three different prices in three different stores located in different areas. To draw valid conclusions, you should choose stores that have similar customer characteristics.

This method works well for established products and provides reliable information. This method, like the other two, has some limitations. Changing economic situations, an increase in competitive advertising, or aggressively lower prices by the competition make the information less valuable.

4. Setting a Price

The following framework shows a number of factors that should be useful when setting a price:

(a) Define the different market segments that you intend to serve and the benefits sought by each one.

(b) Define your corporate strategy. Pricing must be consistent with corporate strategy. A target market share strategy is likely needed if your corporate strategy is to gain market share. Product choices and pricing levels need to be consistent with overall corporate objectives.

(c) Estimate price elasticity. Even a crude estimate is helpful. Sales volumes, profits, and consumer price sensitivity are highly related.

(d) Develop product position. What unique advantage do you have over your competition? How different is your product from that of the competition? Competitors provide the benchmark for pricing. If your product is the same or very similar, you will have to match your competitor's price.

(e) Decide on the appropriate services, distribution channels, and promotion. Identify clearly how you differ from your competitor in terms of the service you provide, such as 24-hour delivery, full warranty, or technical support. What image do you intend to convey? You need to estimate costs to make the right decisions. With value-added service, you may be able to justify a higher price.

(f) Estimate specific cost. Use a reality-based cost system — a system that reflects and allocates real costs, as opposed to a percentage allocation (which is based on an existing cost system) to determine the specific cost related to each product category. Overhead allocation such as research and development or plant investments must be based on actual costs.

(g) Estimate competitors' price orientation. Determine the competitors' possible reaction to new product features or a price change. Competitors react differently depending on their corporate objectives, product and service similarity, fixed costs, operating margins, production flexibility and capacity, financial situation, and established customer loyalty.

(h) Analyze environmental factors. What legal requirements must you meet? What industrial practices could restrain your pricing strategy?

(i) Set optimal price. The price must be consistent with the above factors. Pricing is an ongoing concern. Implement a tracking system to measure price performance.

(j) Develop a practical price structure. Decide on a base price to use, and what terms, discounts, allowances, rebates, and incentives to apply. Your price structure should vary by the type of transaction in order to maximize profits. Recognize that customers are influenced by different price incentives. Keep your pricing structure simple to facilitate implementation and enhance customer comprehension.

When setting price, psychological factors also need to be considered. Image pricing is effective for ego-sensitive products such as luxury cars, perfumes, or special treats. Although there may be no relationship between a higher price and quality, people usually associate quality with higher prices. Buyers perceive odd number pricing favorably for low price products.

Pricing is one part of your overall revenue generating strategy. Price strategy should be related to product performance and corporate strategy. The above framework represents a common base for discussions to set price based on your products' perceived value relative to the competition.

The questions that follow can help you analyze your price structure and arrive at a pricing strategy.

QUESTIONS

1. What are your pricing objectives? Have you determined whether to price below, at, or above the market?

_____
_____
_____
_____
_____
_____

2. What are the industry pricing standards?

_____
_____
_____
_____
_____
_____
_____

3. Can you offer trade-ins, free accessories, or free service rebates?

_____
_____
_____
_____
_____
_____

4. Do you offer deferred billing, discounts for cash payment, or early payment?

_____
_____
_____
_____
_____
_____

5. How do market forces affect your pricing strategy?

_____

_____

_____

_____

_____

_____

_____

6. Are you influenced by competitors' price changes? What does the competition charge? Is there price cutting?

_____

_____

_____

_____

_____

_____

_____

7. What is your average cost per unit? Have you set specific markups for each product? Do you set prices to cover full costs on every sale or do you have loss leaders?

_____

_____

_____

_____

_____

_____

_____

8. Do you plan discounts for quantity purchases, special groups, or seasonal sales?

_____

_____

_____

_____

_____

_____

_____

8
ADVERTISING

Your advertising strategy is a means of communicating to customers how your product helps them satisfy their goals. The primary task of advertising is to provide information, reinforcement, or assurance. Advertising rarely creates sales unless you have a product that benefits a large group of people.

Advertising can encourage immediate buying action and generate traffic for retail purchase by attracting new dealers, distributors, and customers. It delivers useful information to customers, encourages them to try out a new product, and provides you with an ongoing contact that may serve to maintain interest after sales by confirming customers' purchase decisions. It promotes new uses and features of your product, creates a company personality, and encourages product loyalty. Advertising can also complement your salespeople's objectives and presentations and may even help open doors for them.

1. Advertising Campaign

You must decide exactly what advertising should do for your company. The following summary outlines your first considerations when planning an effective advertising campaign.

1.1 Target market

Consumers are exposed to up to 1,500 messages per day; therefore, most people notice those ads that meet their needs and ignore those that do not trigger an interest.

For an ad to be noticed and successful, you have to match your product with customers' needs. You must decide who your potential market is and find out where they are located. What are their incomes? Do they live in apartments or houses? What are their levels of education, types of occupation, and ages? What are their living and shopping habits? Which media do they listen to or read? How do they use the product? How often do they use it? Who tends to buy the product: men, women, or both? Before you decide what to say and where to place your ad, you must know to whom you are talking. Research can help.

1.2 Market research

The market research data you gathered using the techniques discussed in Chapter 5 will help you pinpoint your target market. You must also study what the competition is doing, which attributes of your product are important, and how your product is both similar to and different from its competition.

Research can help you understand what is important to your customers so you can tell them what they want to know and hear. For example, one study indicated that when evaluating a particular import car, consumers said that the factors important to them included the car's gas mileage, manufacturer, reputation, and quality of workmanship. But the features mentioned by the salesperson during the sales presentation were the car's gas mileage, its roominess, front wheel drive, and ease of driving. Except for gas mileage, all the other points communicated by the salesperson about the car were not important to the customer.

1.3 Advertising objectives

Your advertising objectives should be carefully defined for each particular advertisement as well as for the whole advertising campaign.

Advertising objectives usually fall into three main categories.

(a) *Information:* Describes your product features and benefits, where you are located, your price, and response to service enquiries.

(b) *Persuasion:* Proclaims the advantages of your product and tries to convince the customer to buy.

(c) *Reminder:* Reminds potential customers of your products and their benefits.

1.4 Message development

Much can be said about your product, but advertising should emphasize one theme. Businesses often lose their focus and stop stressing the benefits that made them famous and successful. For example, many cough and cold products seek to become cure-alls for cold congestion, the flu, allergies, and hay fever. A cold remedy company could increase its share of the market substantially by using a simple ad that emphasizes the product as a special medication designed only to clear your nose.

You should know exactly what it is you want to say and why you're saying it. Messages to your target audience can be developed in many ways. The best approach is the one dictated by customers. Intuition and inspiration are valuable tools for the creation of a message, but should be tried out on potential customers.

1.5 Message potency

The impact or potency of your message depends on these three criteria:

(a) *Desirability:* You must appeal to people's self-interests and needs such as health, security, prosperity, approval, attraction, or comfort.

(b) *Exclusivity:* Many ads try to appeal to people's self-interests. For your ad to be noticed, it must be distinct; it must attract people's attention and be recognizable. Your message must be consistent with your image and market position.

Exclusivity or distinctiveness is often associated with creativity. But beautiful messages by themselves do not fulfill your advertising objectives. Your advertisement should clearly differentiate your product from the competition.

(c) *Believability:* You have the customer's attention. Now you must make your claim believable. In advertising, credibility may be the most difficult element to control. That's why informal sources such as friends and neighbors or testimonials from credible sources have a strong influence. Since your goal is to make a profit as a business, your credibility is based on factors such as your company's past performance, the quality of product, your image, your reputation and choice of distribution outlets, your social responsibility in the community, and the media you are using to advertise your product.

2. Media Selection

Which media are used by your target audience: newspaper, television, radio, magazine, Internet, email, or direct mail? What are the advantages and disadvantages of each medium? What type of media mix is appropriate for your product?

You need to answer these questions as you explore the possibilities for advertising your product. For example, if you own a convenience store, most of your customers come from your immediate neighborhood, so the best medium could be the community newspaper. If you are selling heavy machinery to a contractor, you may want to use magazine ads or direct mail.

Further, to make a strong impression, you must have the right balance between reach and frequency. Reach is the total number of individuals exposed to your message. Frequency is the number of times each person is exposed to your message. If you have a small target market, frequency is more important than reach. Television is a very expensive means of advertising, but has a high reach, while radio is less expensive and has a high frequency. What counts is the cost-per-thousand to the right audience rather than the total cost.

Consumers forget advertising, which is why repetition is so important. One study showed that public awareness of an advertisement in several magazines was an average of 19 percent after one exposure and 37 percent after three exposures. On the radio, 50 to 100 advertisements per week for 6 to 13 weeks is the recommended frequency to saturate your audience.

2.1 Newspapers

Life without newspapers is hard to imagine. Locally produced, the newspaper is an accepted and important part of community life. To the customer, the newspaper is immediate, practical, important, and, to a great extent, authoritative.

Newspapers primarily reach adults with above-average incomes and education. They serve local markets and concentrated populations. They are good for special promotions, grand openings, and for communicating something that must be known immediately.

Newspapers are flexible; you can run an advertisement of any size at any time of the week in any section of the paper. You can select your audience by advertising in specific sections such as the sports, business, or fashion sections. The short closing date of newspapers allows advertisers to make last-minute changes or to cancel on a few days' notice. Newspapers are timely and the North American public prefers advertising in newspapers to that found in any other medium.

Newspapers provide intense coverage of the local market and provide sufficient room to explain complex messages. Most metropolitan newspapers have special geographic editions allowing circulation in the desired market area. Pass-along readership is estimated to average 2 to 2.5 readers per edition.

On the other hand, newspapers have a short lifespan, poor color reproduction, many ads to compete with, and a confusing rate structure. Further, people in their twenties (and younger), a large group of consumers, read newspapers less often than others.

2.2 Magazines

Magazine readers tend to have higher incomes and higher education levels. Magazines aim for specific groups of people with common tastes and interests such as tradespeople, business owners, farmers, professionals or managers, sailors, golfers, or home renovators. Each magazine has a different reputation, prestige, credibility, cost, and market profile. New medical equipment, for example, would best be advertised in a medical journal. An executive briefcase would best be advertised in a business magazine such as *The Wall Street Journal, Business Week*, or *The Financial Post Magazine*.

Magazines can accommodate ads for products that require a lengthy explanation. They have good color reproduction and high-quality printing. Because the pass-along readership of consumer magazines is estimated to average over three readers per copy, magazines have a longer life and can reach a local or a national market. Your business image can be enhanced by association with a prestigious magazine.

There are limitations, however. The lead time before publication is longer, which limits flexibility and detracts from the urgency and immediacy of an ad's impact. Since magazines are more focused than newspapers, you probably won't get a wide circulation among audiences of all ages, incomes, and levels of education. (There are exceptions, like *TV Guide*.)

2.3 Radio

To gain a share of the market, radio stations specialize in their programs, newscasters, and music by tailoring their programming to selective audience segments. In comparison with television, radio influence is mainly at the local or regional level.

Obviously, the audience is related to the type of program. Rock music appeals to teens; country and western music generally appeals to the blue-collar sector; Top 40 tunes appeal to the young and single.

Radio is very flexible and easily accessible. You can buy air time any time of the day and you can select your audience. Radio is a companion, so you can reach people while they're driving or doing housework. Radio allows listeners to use their imaginations and have a one-to-one relationship with the announcer. It is dynamic. Radio's local aspect allows identification with a region.

Radio is easier to tune out than other media. There is the danger that if too many commercials air in sequence, your message will be harder for listeners to recall.

2.4 Television

Almost 98 percent of all homes in North America have a television set, and the average family spends about six hours a day watching television. This means you can reach more people at one time than with any other medium.

The markets you can reach via television vary with the time of day. Television audiences can be broken into 14 distinct segments, characterized by leisure interests and common needs.

Three of the segments contain a heavy concentration of adult men, four contain a heavy concentration of adult women, three include primarily young people, three include a balance of both adult men and women, and one consists of older, family-oriented men who live in suburban and rural areas. Each segment watches different television programs; your product should be advertised during those shows that are watched by your target audience.

By using television, you can reach a large audience either locally, regionally, or nationally. It is the most dynamic medium because it appeals to the senses of both sight and hearing, and can therefore dramatize spoken words. Television is excellent for demonstrating the uses and benefits of a service. However, for most businesses, television advertising is usually affordable only on a local basis, and the problem of many ads being aired together reduces advertising recall. Back-to-back competitive commercials creates a serious loss in advertising effectiveness.

2.5 Internet or email

The Internet has a growing number of users. Most people have email these days too. Chapter 12 will cover this in detail.

2.6 Direct mail

Direct mail is advertising literature that is sent through the postal system. A broadcast or a print ad mentions only highlights of your story. In contrast, direct mail tells your whole story.

The advantages of direct mail are many. Direct mail allows you to control where your literature is distributed. You can develop your own mailing lists or buy suitable ones from other organizations. Direct mail can be personalized to the needs of that particular group or addressed to a specific individual. The message is not restricted by space limitations; you can include as much detail about your product as you think appropriate or necessary. The timing of the advertising is completely under your control.

Your message is not competing with other advertisers. Response to a direct mail advertising campaign can be more precisely measured than is possible in other media. Depending on many factors, approximately one to four percent of direct mail recipients will respond to your offer. Direct mail can be tailored to fit almost any budget and can easily test variations of your messages.

The disadvantage of direct mail is that it lacks the prestige of magazine, radio, newspaper, and television advertising. Many people call this type of advertising "junk mail" and don't bother reading it.

2.7 Media mix

Using more than one medium can be beneficial if you use the same theme. When people read a newspaper advertisement, then hear a radio spot with the same theme, it helps reinforce the message. Advertising and media selection should be consistent with your customers' needs and interests. Try an advertisement and see what happens. Track the ad's effectiveness. Make sure you evaluate the media audiences and characteristics against your market and company strategies and goals. Keep in mind your target market, type of product, message, and cost.

3. Timing

Keep in mind that sales opportunities are lost when advertising is too late or too early; marketers try to time their advertising when interest is high. For example, Halloween costume rentals are most popular before November 1. Ski outlets start advertising in autumn when skiers' thoughts turn to the slopes. Food stores distribute their flyers throughout their neighborhoods or place an ad in the newspaper on Wednesdays and Thursdays prior to weekend shopping.

4. Message Execution

No matter which medium, or combination of media, you choose, how you present yourself and your product is very important. A fine French champagne served in a plastic mug would lose some of its appeal. The style, tone, and elements such as color, size, and type of illustration and copy all influence how your message is perceived.

Consider the following points when preparing your advertising message.

4.1 Headline

Your headline must capture your audience's attention. Approximately five times as many people read a headline as read the copy. If the headline doesn't grab the reader, the advertiser may have just lost a customer. To be most effective, your headline should —

- Be specific and tell customers how they will benefit if they continue to read the ad

- Give news, command, or ask a question

- Reveal something of interest and be intriguing to the customer

- Include your brand name, and if you're advertising in the local newspaper, the city's name

- Be in boldface type and not end with a period

4.2 Copy

Copy is the printed message. The purpose of the copy is to elaborate on the headline, to sell, inform, heighten interest, offer proof, or move someone to action. A good copywriter has empathy with the intended audience's point of view.

Your opening paragraph should be short. Get to the point. Get the major idea of the ad across quickly and repeat it several times. Be sure it is clear.

Use sub-headings and describe what your product offers and for whom it is intended.

Give facts, information, confirmations, and justifications. Be specific and use clear language. Use persuasive, active words; avoid language that sounds stilted and monotonous.

Talk directly to the customer. The copy should be personal. Where possible, show the expected result from using your product. Focus on one theme, one subject, one person.

Create desire by giving your customer an excuse to buy. Tell your reader how to acquire your product. Ask for the order. Emotion, humor, and fear work under limited conditions. Repeat your brand name several times. People are offended by advertising that insults their intelligence or patronizes them. Use good taste. Be certain to include the name, address, and telephone number of your business and the hours of operation.

4.3 Layout

The layout deals with the position of the headline, subheads, pictures, price, type of copy, company logo, address, and telephone number. The layout should guide the eye from one element to the next and keep the reader's interest.

Choose illustrations, copy, and a typeface that convey the desired mood. The layout should first direct the reader's attention to the principal idea, then to subordinate elements. It must present the basics in a simple, unified, and cohesive form.

An ad can appear formal, active, or informal depending on whether the elements are presented symmetrically or asymmetrically. Color or white space can be used to direct attention to illustrations, special features, key charts, or headlines.

A picture is often the first and only thing people notice, so it should show the product in use. Do not include a picture if it is for decoration only. If you use photographs of a person, use someone your audience can identify with. Quality pictures work better than drawings, and under most conditions, four-color ads attract more attention than those in black and white. Your ad layout and typesetting should be consistent with your other ads and with your company image.

A customer questions a product's reliability if all the relevant information is not available. If you don't give your customers the information they need, they manufacture their own "information." To avoid misinterpretation about your offer, give your audience all the information they need.

5. Advertising Budget

Think of advertising as an investment rather than as an expense. The task method and the mechanical method are two common techniques of determining an advertising budget.

5.1 Task method

To determine your advertising budget, develop your advertising objectives, then enumerate the tasks required to attain those objectives and estimate the cost of each. The total advertising budget is determined by adding together the expense of each task. Eliminate the least important duties if you cannot afford to accomplish them all. Avoid underinvesting, however, or your advertising cost may not be justified by its benefit.

5.2 Mechanical method

With this method, the budget is based on past cost, which could be a percentage of sales or a figure equal to what the competition is investing. On the average, the overall industry budget benchmark is approximately three percent of gross sales. The mechanical method is a simple budget method, but it ignores the profit potential of a well-planned advertising campaign.

The minimum that should be invested in advertising varies among industries depending on the nature of the offer, the market, and what the competition is doing, but don't spread your advertising dollars too thin over too many advertising vehicles.

It is important that your company and the ad agency agree on mutual roles and expectations. More money spent on advertising does not guarantee more sales. A good-looking, expensive idea is not the same as a good ad.

As a guideline you should allow for a fairly large advertising budget if your business does not have a large base of regular customers, if it has high inventory turnover and low markups, if it is a fairly new business, or if it faces stiff competition.

On the other hand, if you are well established with a lot of repeat customers, or if you have low inventory turnover and high markups, you need to spend relatively little on advertising. To help you evaluate your advertising needs, see "Advertising" on the CD-ROM.

6. Sales Promotions

Sales promotions are a nonpersonal form of selling. They are designed to increase sales, build store traffic, encourage a trial of your product, extend the selling seasons, and support your advertising.

Persuasive promotions such as samplers, coupons, contests, premiums, price reductions, gifts, and special displays are designed to invite customers to buy now. They increase the perceived value of the product by offering something extra.

The impact of your promotion depends on the type and size of your offer and the ease of accepting it. The sales promotion's goals should be to attract new customers, reward existing customers, and inform people of new products.

Sales promotions appeal especially to price-conscious consumers and to existing customers. Immediate sales response can be high in the short run, but often leaves little permanent gain. For sales promotions to be effective, combine them with your advertising and personal selling efforts. When combining a promotion with advertising, recall and persuasion can be greatly enhanced.

However, for promotional advertising to be effective, it should not detract from the advertising copy, and both the advertising copy and promotional offer should have the same objective and be consistent with your product image.

7. Legal Dos and Don'ts When Advertising

To minimize potential problems or claims of misleading advertising, the following advertising cautions should be understood and complied with by the business owner and any employees:

- Don't use illustrations that are different from a description of the product actually being sold.

- Don't use the term "regular price" in an advertisement unless it is the price at which the product is usually sold.

- Don't run a sale for a long period or repeat the sale every week.

- Don't increase the price of the product to cover the cost of a free product or service.

- Don't use the words "sale" or "special" unless a significant price reduction has occurred.

- Don't confuse regular price with manufacturer's suggested list price, as they are often not the same.

- Don't overuse disclaimers.

- Don't make a performance claim before you can substantiate it, even if you think it is accurate.

- Don't forget that no one actually needs to be misled in order to convince the court that an advertisement is misleading.

- Don't sell a product above your advertised price.

- Don't forget that the legislation protecting the public covers the naive as well as the sophisticated consumer.

- Do avoid terms or phrases in an advertisement that are not meaningful or clear to the ordinary person.

- Do fully and clearly disclose all material that is important and relevant information in the advertisement.

- Do ensure that you have reasonable quantities of a product advertised at a bargain price.

- Do ensure that your sales force is familiar with the law in terms of representations. An advertiser may be held responsible for representations made by its employees.

9
PUBLIC RELATIONS

Public relations is a useful marketing tool and a relatively low-cost method of enhancing your firm's image and credibility. It is a means of communicating or telling your business story.

Public relations is often equated with "fire fighting" or explaining and defending certain incidents or practices. However, public relations is more effective if it is proactive rather than reactive, which for most businesses consists of open-door communication. Talk to your employees, customers, suppliers, banker, government agent, professional and trade associations, and media representatives. Find out what they think about your business and product. Are you perceived as reliable? Do they think you treat your customers well? Are you a good corporate citizen? Do you provide good value? Are the products and related services you provide consistent with your advertising? Is your advertising done in good taste?

After talking to a wide sector of people, you can determine what you need to do to change public perception, and what you need to continue doing to maintain or achieve your desired image.

1. Publicity

One way to communicate your image is through a publicity program. Publicity can often be obtained when you implement a change. Perhaps you are introducing a new product or a modification to a standard product. Or perhaps you can focus on your move to a new location, a unique employee program, or a contest.

Publicity is the art of getting the media to carry a news story about you without your having to pay for it. The objective behind a publicity campaign is to contact members of the media and convince enough of them to run your story to impress your market.

To contact the media you need a media kit, which usually contains a cover letter, a news release, a fact sheet, a sample product, and perhaps a customer list (especially if you are well-established and have some high-profile customers). The most important part of your media kit is your news release. Follow these guidelines for writing a successful news release:

(a) The first paragraph should answer the important questions of who, what, where, when, why, and how.

(b) Deal with facts, not opinions. Make sure the information is well-written and accurate.

(c) Always identify the author of the news release, the name of your organization, the contact person, and telephone number.

(d) Use short, punchy sentences with action verbs.

(e) Do not carry incomplete sentences over to the next page. Always start each page with a new paragraph.

(f) Always date the news release.

(g) Type it double-spaced, and leave wide margins.

(h) Don't go beyond two pages if possible.

(i) At the end of the news release, type "—30—" or "END."

Keep in mind that a news release should be short and to the point. The first paragraph should summarize the whole story; the remaining paragraphs should elaborate. If a newspaper decides to run your news release, it may or may not print the entire piece. If it is cut, the editor works from the last paragraph to the first, so you want the most important information at the beginning. It is imperative that your news release be truthful, accurate, clear, and interesting to read. For an example, see the news release shown in Sample 2.

2. Dos and Don'ts

However you decide to develop your publicity program, make sure what you have to say is news. Answer these questions:

- Is your story unusual?

- Is it topical and newsworthy?

- Will it interest a large number of people?

- Is it of importance to the city (town, region) as a whole?

Create your own media contact list by calling television and radio stations and local newspapers and asking for the name of the person to whom you should send your news releases. Once your kit is complete, call the appropriate person in advance so he or she is prepared for your letter or news release. Include a covering letter that explains why you feel the topic of the presentation is of interest to the readers, viewers, or listeners. Also provide a fact sheet that includes relevant background information about your business, its place and hours of operation, and information about your product.

Make sure all media receive your news release at the same time. It is a good idea to call the day after the news release has been distributed to make sure all contacts received the information and to answer any questions they may have. If you discover an error in your news release after it has been released, call the media immediately to correct it.

Have photographs available for media use. They may not be necessary, but they may come in handy. Some media send their own photographer if they want a picture.

SAMPLE 2
NEWS RELEASE

Water Widgets Co.
1234 Inventors Drive
Productville, Anywhere
(555) 555-5555

FOR IMMEDIATE RELEASE

Date: May 1, 20--

Contact: Jane Doe
Communications Director
(555) 555-5555
Local 555

TECHNOLOGICAL BREAKTHROUGH GUARANTEES SAFE DRINKING WATER

On May 15, 20--, a scientific breakthrough in water purification technology will be unveiled by Water Widgets Co. The revolutionary water purifier, called UFO H2O, will be demonstrated to the public on Saturday, at 1234 Inventors Drive, at 10:00 a.m.

The water purifier, invented by Dr. Walter Widget, can extract toxic waste residues, heavy metals, chemicals, and other impurities at 100 percent efficiency.

Large models for industrial use will be available from the manufacturer in June. Hardware stores throughout North America will carry a smaller, inexpensive model ideal for homes. Both models have passed the many stringent government testing requirements.

In a time of greater public awareness and concern over the purity of drinking water, this device will be of great benefit to the community. As Dr. Widget says, "The invention of this device has been the accumulation of my lifelong dream to develop a system to help others enjoy the purity and beauty of natural water."

— 30 —

If you are being interviewed, plan your responses to anticipated questions so your message comes through loud and clear. The interviewer may tell you ahead of time when the story is likely to be used. If not, wait a couple of days and then make a follow-up call to the interviewer. During the course of the conversation, he or she will likely volunteer the information.

If the coverage given to you is not to your liking, call the person responsible and calmly present your side of the story. This often quickly clears up any misunderstanding. If negative comments are made about you and the media asks your opinion, don't hesitate to positively and constructively tell your side of the story. People want to hear both sides.

Send a thank-you note to all media afterward. They appreciate it and it will keep the doors open for you in the future.

Remember that publicity is not limited to the print media. Talk shows on radio and television are constantly on the watch for newsworthy topics for their listeners or viewers. Be certain to address your media kit to the talk show host personally.

And, finally, realize that media response to your campaigns may not be overwhelming! Be persistent and your efforts will pay off.

3. Differences between Publicity and Advertising

Publicity is often confused with advertising. They are most easily differentiated through these broad definitions:

(a) Advertising is the paid use of a medium by an identified sponsor to present a sales message to a mass audience.

(b) Publicity is typically a favorable news presentation made in print, or on radio or television and is not paid for by the organization benefiting from it.

Sample 3 compares the advantages and disadvantages of advertising versus publicity. The following questions can help you decide which approach works best in your situation.

For more information on publicity, see *Getting Publicity*, another title in the Self-Counsel series.

SAMPLE 3
ADVERTISING VERSUS PUBLICITY

ADVERTISING	PUBLICITY
(a) **Control of message** You control the content, style, and timing of your message. If the wording needs to be very specific to communicate effectively, use advertising.	You relinquish much of the control of what is finally said and when the message is conveyed.
(b) **Credibility** People tend to view advertising with some caution.	When a message is presented by a third party, it is perceived as objective, neutral, and therefore credible.
(c) **Intermediaries** No one intervenes between your message and potential customer. If you need to get to your target market with certainty, use advertising.	You must first persuade an editor or producer to print or broadcast your message.

(d) Appearance

May be perceived as hard-sell.

Not perceived as intrusive.

(e) Repetition

You may run the same ad hundreds of times.

Your message is considered news and will be mentioned only once.

(f) Context

Allows you to describe your product and its benefits in more positive and persuasive terms.

Must be presented in a factual way and limits the explanation of the benefits to the customer.

(g) Message type

To be effective, needs to be focused on one clear-cut theme or message per ad.

You can build on overall image which is used by the customer to evaluate a specific appeal.

(h) Communication vehicles

Limited to the formal print and electronic communication channels.

Communication vehicles are virtually endless. For example, you can appear on talk shows, at seminars, and at special events.

(i) Message content (simple versus complex)

Because advertising space is expensive you must keep your message simple, brief, and easy to understand.

Publicity allows you to explain complex ideas with many examples.

(j) Cost

Considerably more costly than public relations publicity.

Can often be arranged at little or no cost.

QUESTIONS

1. Is your advertising budget large enough to accomplish the job?

   _____
   _____
   _____
   _____

2. Is your headline noticeable? Does it relate to a benefit? Does your copy provide simple, direct information?

   _____
   _____
   _____
   _____

3. What are the objectives of your advertising program? What do you want to communicate? Are you appealing to human interest?

_____
_____
_____
_____
_____
_____
_____
_____

4. If you are going to hire agents to do advertising or public relations for you, have you checked their credentials, seen samples of their previous work, and talked to their clients? Are you comfortable with the advertising campaign offered?

_____
_____
_____
_____
_____
_____

5. Does your advertising and promotion fluctuate with demand? Are certain times and days of the week better than others?

_____
_____
_____
_____
_____
_____

6. How do your advertising plans compare to your competitors? How do you plan to measure the success of the various promotional and advertising programs you are using?

_____
_____
_____
_____
_____
_____

7. What combination of media do you plan to use for maximum impact?

_____
_____
_____
_____
_____
_____

8. Is active demonstration required to best promote your product (e.g., do you need television)?

_____
_____
_____
_____
_____

9. Which radio station, television program, newspaper, or magazine can most effectively reach your target market?

_____
_____
_____
_____
_____

10. Can you make use of direct mail? Have you got a good mailing list? How do you compile a mailing list?

_____
_____
_____
_____
_____

11. Are you using all possible public relations and media available? In what ways?

_____
_____
_____
_____
_____
_____

12. In what ways are you encouraging word-of-mouth referrals?

_____

_____

_____

_____

13. What is your system for promptly answering customer letters or complaints?

_____

_____

_____

_____

14. Does your system acknowledge new customers? Are they generated by your staff through public relations? How?

_____

_____

_____

_____

15. Which relevant community groups, associations, clubs, boards, and committees should you or your staff be a part of?

_____

_____

_____

_____

16. Do you have brochures or fact sheets for customers who wish for additional information? Do you update the information?

_____

_____

_____

_____

10

DISTRIBUTION: GETTING THE PRODUCT TO YOUR CUSTOMER

A great product benefits no one unless you can make it available to your customer. The goal of any distribution system is to bring your goods to your target market.

The key to successful distribution is to make your product available at a time and place that is convenient to your target market. Success comes from making it easy for the customer to buy. Many entrepreneurs make millions by simply changing or improving on distribution.

1. Methods of Distribution

There are four common approaches to bringing goods to customers.

1.1 Producer-to-customer

The simplest and most direct marketing channel is from the producer to the customer. This approach avoids potential conflicts that may arise between producers and wholesalers or between wholesalers and retailers.

As a producer, you do not have to go through lengthy negotiations, contracts, or compromises. You have direct contact with the customer and provide the services required. If you have a new product or you are starting a new business, sometimes it may be the only way to sell your goods. Let's look at a few examples of this approach.

1.1.a Open markets

Perhaps one of the oldest and simplest ways to sell your product is at the market: flea markets, fish markets, or meat and fresh produce markets. To sell at a market, telephone the organizer and arrange to rent a booth. On the day of the market, arrive early with your goods, set the booth up with an attractive display, and sell.

1.1.b Door-to-door

Vacuum cleaners, cosmetics, encyclopedias, and cookbooks are some of the more popular products that are sold door-to-door. Some computer companies have also found it profitable to sell this way. Door-to-door selling requires methodical planning. You need to hire sales staff, prepare a standard presentation and demonstration, and designate territories to each salesperson.

1.1.c Trade shows

Most industries hold a trade show every year. At these shows, you might be able to contact industrial buyers who otherwise might not have the time to see you. During the show, make sure that your staff is energetic, easy-to-approach, alert, and talkative with prospective customers. Exchange business cards, distribute literature on your product, and follow up these contacts in writing.

1.1.d Street vending

Street vending is an excellent way to sell fresh-cut flowers, popcorn, crafts, hot dogs and fries, T-shirts, lottery tickets, special event tickets, and ice cream. It does require that you pick appropriate routes and territories. You also need to check with the local authorities if you need a license and if there are any regulations you need to adhere to.

1.1.e Product inserts

Inserts are product brochures or coupons enclosed in the package of a related product. Let's say you are selling small batteries, for example. You could include coupons or order forms in the box of a popular children's toy to promote them. The advantages of package inserts are cost savings, the ability to target your market directly without the expense of postage, and

gained credibility by associating with another credible company.

1.1.f Home party

All kinds of products, from pictures to lingerie, are being sold at home parties. You begin by having a small group of friends in your own home. You make your sales presentation and then everyone is free to try on or examine the goods. Afterward, when everyone is enjoying refreshments, you can retire to the kitchen to write up orders. By offering incentives to your guests, you can book similar parties where there will be new guests who may be interested in booking even more parties with you.

1.1.g Government

The range of goods that governments buy, at all levels, is very wide. To sell your product to government, contact the department most likely to buy from you. They will advise you on the appropriate procedure to follow to make sure you are considered for contracts. The process may be long and involved, but the benefits can be significant since government is such a large purchaser.

1.2 Producer-to-retailer-to-customer

Traditional examples of producer-to-retailer-to-customer distribution include large department stores or specialty shops that buy directly from the producer. You should also consider vending machines where all kinds of products from jelly beans to jeans are being sold profitably. Or, you may wish to try selling your product on consignment. Here are some examples of this distribution approach.

1.2.a Department stores

Major department stores have buying departments in their head offices. You can call to determine which buyer you should be talking to and when you can meet. Show your full line of products and be able to demonstrate them. The buyer may be interested in seeing a business plan, market research, and evidence of a sound, well-run company. The advantage of this approach is that after you have made the initial sale, distribution to all the department store's retail outlets is handled by the store itself.

This technique can also be used in chain and discount stores. Approaching major department stores can sometimes be awkward. You may consider hiring a professional sales agent to approach department stores on your behalf.

1.2.b Manufacturer's sales representatives

A manufacturer's sales representative is an independent salesperson who distributes products to retailers. This salesperson works for you as if you had your own sales staff, but without the overhead costs.

Contracts with your manufacturer's sales representative should include an exclusivity agreement, each party's responsibilities, the amount of the advertising allowance, territories to be covered, billing, return policies, warranties, and commissions.

1.2.c Rack jobbing

Rack jobbing is a good way to give your product exposure and wide distribution at little expense to you. Pantyhose, sunglasses, chewing gum, magazines, and newspapers are usually sold this way. As a producer, you provide retailers with your product free of charge and pay them a commission on sales. In return, the retailer provides you with either shelf space or floor space and gives you the exposure you require free of charge.

1.3 Producer-to-wholesaler-to-retailer-to-customer

Small producers sell to wholesalers who then sell to small retailers. This approach allows indirect contact between thousands of producers and retailers which otherwise would not be economically feasible. Most convenience stores, local pharmacies, hardware stores, and mom-and-pop stores fall into this category.

As an apple grower, for instance, you know that one or two stores cannot handle all your produce by themselves. So you sell your crop by the truckload to a wholesaler who then crates it and ships it to dozens of retailers. You have only one invoice to handle and none of the headaches of dealing with many small retailers.

A variation of this approach is if you have a product that you want manufactured for you. The task, then, is to find a manufacturer who is not only capable of making your product, but is interested in doing so. You have to make sure the production facilities, staff, equipment, and techniques are suited to your product. It is also important that the distribution network reaches your target market. If you're selling industrial staples, for example, and one manufacturer's network is composed of supermarkets, you will have to search further.

The process of locating a manufacturer and negotiating the terms under which the product is made is a complex one involving contracts, royalties, patents, exclusivity, and other factors. It is essential that you consult a lawyer to advise you in these areas to protect your interests.

1.4 Producer-to-agent-to-wholesaler-to-retailer-to-customer

This distribution channel is used in more elaborate marketing situations. An agent acts as a go-between who negotiates purchases, sales, or both, but does not take title of the goods. An agent can act as a go-between for the producer and the wholesaler, or for the producer and the retailer. An agent's main function is to bring buyers and sellers together. This type of channel is common in the agriculture sector, as well as in the food and textile industries.

2. Distribution Considerations

Which of these distribution approaches is best for your product depends on factors such as your customers' buying patterns and needs, your product's characteristics, go-between commissions, and your company's resources.

2.1 The customer

The most critical area to consider when designing a distribution system is the type of customer you want to sell to.

- *Number of customers:* A go-between may be needed to reach a large number of customers. With few customers, the producer may be able to use his or her own sales force.

- *Purchasing patterns:* For an equal number of customers, if customers buy on a frequent basis, a greater number of go-betweens is required. Cigarettes and sundries fall into this category.

- *Geographic dispersion:* In densely populated areas, producers may set up their own sales outlets, but use go-betweens in less concentrated areas.

2.2 Product characteristics

- *Perishability:* Perishable products such as fresh produce and fashionable goods require a more direct or short distribution route to the end user.

- *Product value:* Products of high value or custom-made products are generally sold directly to the customer. Technical products that require installation, maintenance, and service after purchase are also sold directly to the customer.

- *Convenience goods:* Products such as staples, impulse goods, and emergency supplies require a go-between to give the product maximum exposure.

2.3 The go-between

The selling effort by a go-between (or intermediate between two parties) is usually less intense than if it were done by the producer's sales force. In choosing a go-between, pay attention to who is responsible for promotion, storage, and contacts.

The service provided by the go-between should complement the producer's additional distribution needs. If you want your brand to be compared to the competition's, you may have to use the same distribution system.

2.4 Producer characteristics

- *Financial resources:* A financially weak company may have to find a go-between who can provide services such as an appropriate sales force, storage, and transit costs, which the company cannot afford to provide itself.

- *Company policy:* Companies who want to maintain control of service, promotion, and price have to use a more direct distribution system.

- *Experience with distribution:* A company's management experience in marketing may affect its ability to reach the target market.

2.5 Warehousing

Warehousing not only provides storage but also allows for assembly and preparation for shipping. The strategic location and size of a warehouse can give the customer better service and can also reduce transportation costs. An analysis of warehouse locations, to be done in conjunction with plant location, needs to consider market area, existing transportation facilities, and rates.

2.6 Inventory control

The purpose of inventory control is to maintain enough stock to fill customers' orders accurately and on time. The level of inventory is related to the movement and storage of material. Inventory control analysis tries to balance the cost of maintaining inventory against the cost of ordering inventory.

2.7 Packaging

Packaging is concerned both with the protection and promotion of the product. In preparing goods for shipment, certain packaging specifications and containers may be required by the tariff ruler.

Good packaging can reduce costs by preventing breakage, spoilage, and pilfering. Packaging makes products easier to handle and can provide a useful promotional display.

2.8 Material handling

Material handling is the activity associated with moving products within the various channel members' facilities. Proper equipment and use of storage space can reduce the cost of handling by minimizing losses from spoilage, breakage, and theft. The use of forklifts, pallets, and containers can also reduce damage by combining packages into larger units.

2.9 Order processing

Order processing involves an effective interdepartmental information flow that moves from the customer order, the credit check, processing, assembly, and transportation of the goods to the customer. The transportation manager is responsible for interdepartmental coordination and improving procedures to ensure that the customer receives the goods promptly.

2.10 Transportation

There are five major modes of transportation. Each one has advantages and limitations. Which methods you use depends on the type of product and the level of service you want to provide.

2.10.a Rail

Rail has a flexible and wide variety of services. There are fast freight services, pool cars, diversion in transit, and transit and loading privileges. The cost and speed of transit is moderate compared to the other methods. Rail is well-suited for bulky products.

2.10.b Highway

Trucks provide reliable, fast service. Trucking results in less breakage and rough handling than rail, but is more expensive for long hauls. Trucks are suitable for high-value goods, short hauls, and hard-to-reach markets.

2.10.c Water

Shipping via boat serves a limited number of geographical areas and is slow, but the cost of transportation is the least of all methods of transport. Water transportation is suitable for bulky, low-value, nonperishable material such as iron ore, steel, grain, petroleum, gravel, coal, and sand.

2.10.d Pipeline

Pipelines are used to transport material such as oil, natural gas, and crude oil from plant to market. The cost of transportation is low. Pipelines offer a reliable delivery schedule to very limited geographical areas.

2.10.e Air

Air is the fastest means of transportation and allows the movement of perishable commodities that was not possible years ago. The high cost of air transportation may be offset by other factors such as lower cost packaging, lower inventory cost, and speedy service.

A well-designed distribution system provides flexibility, control, and access to your target market at the lowest cost.

Now, answer the following questions. They can help you analyze your own distribution needs.

QUESTIONS

1. Where and when do your customers want your product? Is it easy for your customer to locate you, purchase your product, and get information?

_____

_____

_____

_____

_____

_____

_____

_____

2. What alternate distribution plans do you have if your present suppliers fail to deliver?

_____

_____

_____

_____

_____

_____

_____

3. What services are offered by your present suppliers? How does this differ from other suppliers?

_____

_____

_____

_____

_____

_____

_____

_____

4. How quickly are orders processed and services rendered? What are the consequences of delayed services?

_____

_____

_____

_____

_____

_____

_____

_____

5. How much inventory do you carry? What is the cost of carrying your inventory? What are the consequences of not having all the items available? Do you lose sales?

_____

_____

_____

_____

_____

_____

_____

_____

11
RETAILING YOUR PRODUCT

Retailing is buying goods from a supplier and selling them to a customer. In making a product, the manufacturer has to decide why people will buy the product and what they want from it. You must ask the same questions in the retail business. Who are your customers? Why do they come to your retail outlet and what service do they expect?

1. Retail Classifications

In this book, retail outlets are categorized based on their method of operation. This system is founded on how customers buy and the way retailers accommodate those purchasing patterns.

1.1 Convenience stores

A convenience store is characterized by an easily accessible location and long hours of operation. Small corner grocery stores and gasoline retailers are the usual types of retailers in this category. Convenience stores depend on frequent purchases and should display popular brands in their heavy traffic areas.

1.2 Large department stores

Department stores attract customers by providing a wide variety of products and services. The larger furniture, food, and household appliance outlets also fall into this category.

Customers shop by comparing price, quality, style, and color. The trading area or location is not as critical for department stores as it is for convenience goods. The strategy is to pay close attention to customer needs, to have a good selection of merchandise, to employ knowledgeable and courteous salespeople, to implement a reasonable credit policy, and to have a well-designed layout. Some department stores, through appropriate decorative display, can appeal to a limited market segment by stressing a certain fashion image.

1.3 Specialty stores

Specialty stores provide a wide selection of goods within a single line of merchandise. Bakeries, car dealerships, boutiques, shoe stores, and sporting goods stores are examples of specialty retailers. They provide expertise, personalized service, reputation, and a distinct personality that aims for the tastes of a specific market segment. If you are a specialty retailer, you need effective inventory control since substitute selling is unlikely.

1.4 Discount retailers

Discount stores offer a reasonable selection of well-known brands at a reduced price with a minimum level of customer service. They count on a low-margin, high-turnover operation. They appeal to price-conscious consumers who are accustomed to self-service. The discount retail strategy is to advertise heavily, putting emphasis on the low price of well-known brands.

1.5 Nonstore retailer

Nonstore retailing provides maximum distribution convenience to the customer. Mail-order sales and door-to-door selling for cosmetics, encyclopedias and insurance are examples.

Another form of merchandising is the house party concept where kitchenware or clothing is sold. These marketing techniques tend to appeal to narrow or scattered markets with products that otherwise might not be available. They also appeal to busy individuals who may not have the time or ability to go shopping, and to those who don't like battling crowds and poor parking facilities.

2. Consumer Motives

Effective retailing strategy pays close attention to the motives of the consumer. Shoppers want to go to a store where they fit in. Generally, customers DO want —

- Price, value, and fairness
- Specialization
- Quality and wide selection
- Courteous salesclerk service and technical assistance
- Convenient location, store hours, and parking facilities
- Pleasant store layout/atmosphere
- Credit billing policies
- Guarantee of exchange
- Adjustment policies
- Delivery service
- Accurate advertising

Customers DO NOT want —

- Limited assortment of merchandise
- Pressure to buy
- Indifferent or discourteous salespeople
- Long wait for service
- False promises
- Overpricing
- Careless wrapping
- Poor ventilation and lighting
- Careless housekeeping

3. Types of Shoppers

Studies have identified seven types of shoppers. Retailing strategies should vary to appeal to these different types.

3.1 Inactive shoppers

Shoppers who have a low interest in shopping are called inactive shoppers. They do not engage in outdoor or do-it-yourself activities except around the house. They are usually older shoppers, primarily women, and have little concern about price, service, or product selection.

3.2 Active shoppers

Active shoppers have a high interest in shopping. They are usually from 10 to 34 years old and enjoy many activities including the outdoors and do-it-yourself projects. Price, quality, fashion, and selection are all important to them.

3.3 Service shoppers

Service shoppers are typically of the middle class with dependent children, and they feel in-store service is most important. They want friendly, helpful, and prompt attention.

3.4 Traditional shoppers

Traditional shoppers enjoy outdoor activities such as camping, fishing, or hunting. They do not particularly enjoy shopping, they are not demanding, and they are not overly concerned with price.

3.5 Dedicated fringe shoppers

Fringe shoppers are the do-it-yourself individualists who are likely to try new products. Showing little brand or store loyalty, they rely heavily on print media as their main source of information and have little interest in radio or television advertising.

3.6 Price shoppers

Composed mainly of older, married, middle-class people, price shoppers are very price sensitive and go out of their way to find a bargain. They rely heavily on all forms of advertising to find the best prices.

3.7 Transitional shoppers

Transitional shoppers are usually young, married, and lower class. They have not firmly established their lifestyles and shopping values. They quietly decide to buy a product and are not price sensitive. They enjoy outdoor activities and their cars.

4. Choosing a Location

Choosing a site in which to locate your retail outlet involves two main decisions. First, is there a need to open a retail outlet or office in the area? Second, within a given geographical area, where specifically should you locate your facilities?

4.1 Choosing an area

You must consider the size of the trading area, the size of the population, and the demographic trends. For example, find out how many one-person households there are. Do people rent or own? Is it mainly industrial or service oriented?

Determine whether the average income in the area is above, equal to, or below the national average so you know what socioeconomic group you would be serving. Find out how much competition exists and its level of quality.

Before you move to an area, consider both the costs and potential revenue. Decide what management structure you need to coordinate and maintain quality control over your new operation.

4.2 Choosing a specific site

Look at the district's attractiveness and appearance. Do your customers prefer a neighborhood or a downtown ambience? There should be appropriate access roads and parking facilities. Can traffic stop at your site without difficulty? How much traffic passes by? See if the adjacent store or office complements your operation. Find the competition's existing location. Do you want your products to be compared? What other potential competition could arise?

You have to take into account zoning regulations, occupancy, lease terms, site maintenance, and utilities. Is there potential for expansion and flexibility for restructuring office layout? Compare the total cost to that of other locations. If you are renting, does the store front or office entrance attract people's attention and invite them to enter? Does it fit your image? Finally, are there washroom facilities, water fountains, and telephones accessible to the public?

The questions on the following pages can help you organize your strategy for retailing your product.

QUESTIONS

1. Which of your items are bought on impulse? Are they easily accessible? Are the price tags easily readable? Do you know which of your items have unusual eye appeal and can be effective in display?

_____

_____

_____

_____

_____

_____

_____

_____

2. Can you foresee changes in the profile of your store's neighborhood? If so, what are they?

_____

_____

_____

_____

_____

_____

_____

3. What is your plan for deciding what to buy and from whom?

    _____
    _____
    _____
    _____
    _____
    _____
    _____
    _____
    _____

4. Have you broken down your merchandise by departments or merchandise classification? Does it help your inventory control? Are you using a unit control system?

    _____
    _____
    _____
    _____
    _____
    _____
    _____
    _____
    _____
    _____

5. How do you keep track of the success of your buying decisions to aid you in next year's buying? Do you evaluate your suppliers' performances?

    _____
    _____
    _____
    _____
    _____
    _____
    _____
    _____

12
MARKETING ON THE INTERNET

Since 1994, the vast network of interconnected host computers has grown by more than 100 percent per year. The Internet is accessible in the United States, Canada, Australia, New Zealand, and most European countries. However, except for Egypt, Zaire, and South Africa, many rural parts of Africa are not yet connected to the Internet. The high-tech Asian countries and regions such as Japan, Hong Kong, Singapore, Taiwan, India, Indonesia, and Malaysia all have access to the Internet.

The Internet began as a military-driven national security project during the Cold War. After the end of the Cold War, the Internet was used mainly by schools, research organizations, and those in computer-related occupations to exchange information. Today, many people still use the Internet for research, but a large number of new users look to the Internet for news, game-playing, socializing, and now for a place to do business.

The percentage of online shopping users compared to the percentage of users for research, education, entertainment, news, information exchange, and socializing is low, though this is changing. Purchasing via the Internet has been driven by convenience and time savings. Surveys indicate that more would have been purchased had the products or services been available. This represents tremendous opportunities for businesses. There are, however, issues that need to be addressed. For instance, many Internet users are deterred from purchasing on the Internet because they do not trust Internet security (discussed in further detail below).

1. Who Will Your Customers on the Internet Be?

The key factor in a successful business enterprise is knowing who your customers are. In

1998, the typical Internet user was a highly educated, Caucasian North American male in his mid-thirties, affluent, and computer literate. The median household income for the Internet user was 65 percent higher than the median household income for the nation. More than one-third of Internet users had an undergraduate degree. This suggested that over the short term, products targeting men would likely fare better than others.

However, this profile of Internet users was misleading because the Internet rapidly evolved toward the mainstream consumer. What the results of most surveys showed was the dramatic growth in the number of women users. The same type of range is also seen in comparisons of age groups and of median salary. Today, many North American households have an Internet connection with people of all ages and demographics using the Internet regularly and with ease.

A more precise description of users is difficult as a result not only of the great number of new Internet users but also of the lack of standardization in research methods. Although numbers and descriptions can provide an overall view of users and the dollars spent on the Internet, they should be interpreted with caution.

In traditional marketing, a business is expected to first segment the target markets, find out where they are, and then aim its marketing efforts toward these prospects. But on the Internet, it is the prospect who takes the initiative to visit a business website: Your advertising is being pulled by the user rather than being pushed onto them. This means that your business needs to be easy to find through search engines; choose as key search words criteria you think are desirable to your potential customers. You need to ask the question, "How will they find me?" rather than, "How do I find them?"

2. Services Internet Customers Expect

Although it is changing, the number of sales transactions over the Internet in comparison to the catalogue industry or to the total industry is extremely small. Online consumers want to make well-informed decisions. They want to be provided with the relevant information and options. They want to feel in control and be able to voice their opinions.

Not all consumers are looking for the same thing. As with other media, you need to think of the Internet as being composed of different market segments. Younger subscribers are more likely to demand more information on music and entertainment and on computer hardware and software. Many baby boomers want information on education, training, health and medicine, and investment opportunities. There are great opportunities for specialized services catering to the mature markets, as well as to special-interest groups. And although we primarily discuss catering to consumer shopping, business-to-business commerce represents substantial potential on the Internet.

To be successful on the Internet, you need to provide useful information and allow for customer interaction and feedback. In addition to relevant information, the consumer is more likely to buy from you if you can provide:

(a) *Better price.* With access to almost anywhere in the world, customers have a lot to choose from. Often, price will dictate which products they will buy.

(b) *Better service.* Customers want to be able to ask questions and get prompt service. You need to be able to anticipate and answer prospects' questions as well as to follow up should customers need help after purchasing your product.

(c) *Convenience.* You need to make it easy for customers to obtain your products. Complicated instructions and forms and long delays in delivery are not satisfactory.

(d) *Easy browsing.* Shopping on your website needs to be easy, fast, and fun for consumers. Long downloading time and complex displays will turn consumers to the competition.

3. What Products Can Be Sold on the Internet?

Certain types of products fare better being sold via the Internet than others. Computers and accessories, software, audio and consumer electronics, airline tickets, hotel accommodations, rcal cstatc, and financial services all sell well on the Internet. The Internet makes it easy for financial institutions to provide services such as summaries of the day's trades, account status, closing prices, and rate of exchange on the dollar.

There have also been success stories in selling books, games, toys, specialty hobbies and crafts, employment services, flowers, clothing, and jewelry. A significant increase is expected in the sale of industrial equipment and parts as more purchasing departments gain the training, the infrastructure, and the experience in accessing the Internet.

For some consumers, the opportunity to browse without feeling pressured gives them a sense of control. For example, many people find themselves anxious when purchasing a car and dislike high-pressure tactics used by salespeople. The Internet search engines allow users to get to a website such as the Dealer Dashboard (www.dealerdashboard.com) to access online information about prices and see color photos of the models, while avoiding sales pressure.

The Internet, like a catalogue, allows shoppers easy access to a great choice of products that may not be available locally. With this global audience, the ideal products and services to sell are those that are more easily accessed via the Internet, including those that require fast and reliable updated information. Your Internet site can offer information such as bulletins, reference sources, statistics, research reports, and government information. This represents tremendous cost-savings in the production of printed booklets and flyers and conventional mailing. News, sports, weather summaries, and special-interest group discussions all provide opportunities to present your business's interest. But you must be careful to do so in a style that is consistent with the Internet culture. There are many good books available about the Internet and "netiquette"; check your local bookstore.

4. Advantages of the Internet

Web advertising can offer increased awareness of your business, easy methods to distribute information, opportunities for text and video presentation, and a direct line between customers and staff, all at a cost lower than traditional methods of performing these marketing tasks. Here are some unique advantages of advertising on the Internet over other traditional advertising methods:

- Advertising can be presented 24 hours a day, 365 days a year.

- Web pages are accessed because of the user's interest.

- Response and results are immediate, measurable, and interactive, which tells you something about the value of your offer and gives you a useful database to focus your marketing efforts.

- You can reach millions of potential customers with minimum distribution and printing fees. The Internet is relatively inexpensive in comparison to other media.

- Material and data on your website is easy to update.

- A small business has the same level of market access as a corporate giant.

5. Is the Internet Right for Your Business?

The Internet has received a lot of attention because of the decreasing cost of powerful hardware, the introduction of user-friendly software, and both positive and negative media coverage. Although the Internet's popularity attracts a lot of attention, opportunities on the Internet must be evaluated just like any other business decision. Many people will always like the social interaction of personal shopping. As well, people want to see, feel, and touch the goods before they buy. This is particularly true for certain types of goods.

Before you begin using the Internet to promote your business, you need to determine if your product fits the Internet environment and whether there is a match between your target customer and the Internet user. You need to establish what your Internet objectives are and determine how much investment you are willing to commit to it. Just because something is new or popular, this does not mean you should automatically adopt it. Your Internet plan should follow the same rigorous analysis as suggested in Appendix 3, The Marketing Plan.

Whether you are considering advertising on the Internet or creating your own website from which visitors can order your products, here are some of the key questions you should ask yourself before you commit:

(a) What do I envision using the Internet for in my business? Is it for improved communication with my customer, to enhance my traditional advertising, to establish a corporate presence, to be associated with new technology, or primarily to get sales?

(b) If it is for sales support, do I have the necessary staff and service support? Have I determined how I will ship my product: electronically or conventionally?

(c) What kind of information and corporate presence do I want to establish?

(d) Do I want to be able to survey my customers and establish a customer research database?

(e) Do I want to have the opportunity to test ads on a regular basis and obtain online demographic data?

(f) Do I want to be able to interact with my customers?

(g) Do I want to establish a customer order tracking system that allows customers to keep current on their accounts and outstanding orders?

(h) Do I want to communicate to my customers product updates, promote new uses, and answer questions?

(i) Do I want to establish personal networking, obtain better business resources, and improve communication with business partners?

(j) Do I want to enhance my business communications by providing inter-office or long-distance communication, and electronic data interchange capabilities?

(k) Do I want my website to act like a global toll-free telephone number for customers, as well as for shareholders and employees?

You also have to consider that although people may not buy via the Internet, they may use the information your website provides before making a purchase at your retail outlet. The information you provide on the web creates a more informed customer.

The Internet makes it easy for your competitors to monitor your offer. Like it or not, the Internet provides a medium where anything can be said about your business. Depending on the validity of what is being said, addressing the issues may mean a change in strategic approach or management style or simply providing honest information about the issues being discussed.

6. Customer Concerns about the Internet

There are three Internet security issues that are subject to ongoing concern: fraudulent use of credit card information, computer security, and information security. The last two concerns are about unauthorized users breaking into computer systems, stealing information, collecting users' passwords, and causing disruption in network activities. Again, there are many resources, from books to computer consultants, that you can turn to if you wish to find out more about these concerns.

Although the chance of someone fraudulently using a credit card number obtained from the Internet is quite low, thanks in part to the increased availability of and improvement in encryption, many people are still anxious about doing business online. You need to inform your customers about the security measures you have undertaken to protect their interests and address their fears. A computer consultant or someone else knowledgeable in the Internet and security (e.g., knowledgeable computer retailers) can help you introduce security measures to protect your customers.

In addition to security matters, Internet users are worried about the reliability of service, the ability to get refunds should products be defective, and the quality of information given over the Internet. The proliferation of junk email, aggressive advertising, and bad publicity is likely to alienate customers and push users away from the Internet. This threat can be greatly reduced by again using proper netiquette.

7. Poor Advertising on the Internet

Businesses in the United States alone are estimated to have spent hundreds of millions to advertise on the Internet. From its beginnings with the military through to its use as a research tool, the Internet has been focused on information. To attract customers, your advertising needs to fit in with this culture. Failure to do so can alienate users and bring about retaliation in the form of email bombing, where your email is inundated with thousands of messages. Like all forms of advertising that is not consistent with the prevailing culture, it will push away potential customers.

If you do not have the expertise, you should consult with an expert before you decide to advertise on the Internet. Here are a few reasons why advertising fails on the Internet:

(a) The advertisement is long and contains too many graphics, which take too long for visitors to your site to download. Remember, there are millions of Internet users with older computers with limited graphic capability and which require long downloading times.

(b) Titles, statements, pages, and text in your advertisement are not properly positioned. How your material will look on screen will vary, depending on what type of computer monitor the viewer is using. There are, however, certain guidelines you can follow to ensure that the majority of viewers will be able to see the material in its best light. Again, an expert in Internet advertising, or one of the many good books available on this subject, can help you in more detail with this.

(c) Failure to include information such as an order form, business phone number, and contact names.

(d) Static billboards (advertisements that don't change and that are not interactive), failure to create a sufficient number of mutual links, and failure to list your website on enough search engines.

As in other forms of advertising, you need to watch for poor spelling and grammar. Your ad should be consistent with your corporate and product image. Make sure you ask for and close the sale. And be sure you have the logistics to handle demand.

Don't forget, advertising on the Internet needs to be combined with the other traditional advertising media. You need to give your Internet address on your business cards, flyers, and advertisements in the Yellow Pages and on television.

8. Website Pitfalls to Avoid

You want your customers to revisit your website often. You should consider some of the reasons that could prevent the customer from wanting to return. What would make you not want to return to a website? Would you revisit a site if the —

- page crashed your browser;

- screen was difficult or impossible to read;

- design or content was ugly or offensive;

- information was useless or inappropriate; or

- content was stale or obsolete?

Did your own list of objections focus on page elements that annoy you: blinking text, too many advertisements, or distracting animations?

The following general principles may help you steer visitors to your site and in the direction you want them to go:

- Most people will follow the first link that appears interesting and, in turn, follow other interesting links. While this may seem obvious, it means that you should position your "important" links first.

- Many people have trouble dealing with pages that rely on "helper applications." A link to a help page doesn't seem to help much.

- No matter how interesting the content, very few people are willing to "sign up" to gain access to a page that requires some form of registration.

- Many people don't like non-black text on a colored background, no matter how aesthetically pleasing it may seem to you.

- Web surfers generally use Microsoft Internet Explorer and/or Mozilla Firefox. Be sure to test your website to make sure it works with both these browsers.

- Opinion seems divided on how often you should change your website's design. Some advocate changing design substantially once or twice a year to keep the look "fresh" and current. However, even if you never redesign your site, it is important that you update your site content often — preferably daily, or at least weekly. On the web, nothing is as stale as yesterday's news. Fresh content will also encourage visitors to "bookmark" your page, for later visits.

These are all worth thinking about, and it is probably safe to say that you can't please everyone. However, after a few months' worth of feedback from visitors to your site, or from a well-chosen "focus group" that can critique the site before it is unveiled to the public, you should have received enough feedback to get a sense of what works and what doesn't.

9. Key Tips to Developing Your Web Marketing

The following website marketing techniques may help you market your product efficiently:

- *Capitalize on trends.* Look for emerging technology trends and quickly capitalize on them.

- *The right tool.* If your customers are asking for Product A and you're spending effort trying to convert them to Product B, you're working too hard. Offer both products and know when to recommend a switch.

- *Overcome objections.* Provide services or systems that integrate more-or-less seamlessly into existing work environments. The message is obvious: Eliminate the reasons people use to justify why they should not choose your product.

- *Focus.* Your core customer base might vary, but it is essential that you stay focused on who they are and what they want.

- *Upgrades and consumables.* For many businesses, it costs about five times as much to acquire a new customer than it does to keep an existing one. Keep that maxim in mind when determining your product line and services.

- *Stop selling bad products.* Damage takes time and money to undo. Some users jump ship and in most cases, they won't return.

- *Lose the "not invented here" mentality.* Start borrowing good ideas from your competitors. Capitalize on the solutions you sell; it's the best possible product demonstration. Think about how Internet services could be incorporated into a customer- or employee-focused solution.

- *Admit mistakes.* When a mistake occurs, be quick to rectify any damage.

- *Hire a marketing whiz.* Hire someone who can look at your Internet needs through a marketing and technical mindset and who has proven expertise and experience.

- *Think again.* Don't be afraid to challenge your deeply held beliefs. Things change quickly. Is this product still the best solution? In what markets are you competitive? Who are your competitors?

- *Understand your audience.* Listen to your customers, understand the values that drive their buying decision, and market products accordingly.

- *Security.* The need for security grows stronger in today's Internet-centric society. Security issues are strong motivators. Hire an Internet security expert to help you implement a secure Internet service for your customers.

10. Key Options to Consider When Marketing Your Website

There are some highly effective options you should consider to ensure that you maximize the marketing benefits of your website. For more information, check out the suggestions from the Medora Research Group. Their website is: www.medora.ca.

10.1 Search Engine Optimization (SEO)

Today, most of us find what we need on the Internet with the help of search engines. Search engines can make a huge difference in the amount of visitors your website receives at any given time, and therefore in the amount of leads your website generates.

The process of optimizing your site to increase the amount of visitors that come from search engines is called Search Engine Optimization (SEO). SEO is a complex topic and is beyond the scope of this book. However, when optimizing your website for search engines, you should:

- Ensure all of your pages are visible to search engines

- Ensure every web page has a unique meta title

- Avoid content duplication

- Make sure that important keywords are present in page name, and/or in your domain name

- Find quality inbound links. For good Google positioning, your website will benefit from quality inbound links (other, reputable websites linking to your pages)

- Create new content frequently!

There are many other factors that can affect your site's positioning in search engines and these factors can change as search engines tweak their search algorithms. We recommend hiring an SEO consultant (do your research here first). In most cases, money paid for SEO is money very well spent.

10.2 Pay-per-click (PPC) campaigns

Pay-per-click (PPC) is online advertising offered by search engines, advertising networks or sites where advertisers only pay when their ad is clicked. The price per click is either a fixed or a variable rate, the latter if a bidding system is used. The top PPC providers are Google AdWords, Yahoo! Search, and Microsoft adCenter.

Although not a search engine, and its ads are not strictly PPC, Facebook, one of the biggest social networking sites, is gaining online market share quickly. Some sources say it is now able to deliver as many ad clicks as Google does.

10.3 Opt-in email marketing and advertising

Email marketing (or e-newsletter marketing), is a form of direct marketing when an email that advertises products or services is sent to an existing or potential list of clients. The "opt-in" means that all of your recipients have previously provided their consent to receive such emails. If no consent has been provided then such messages are called spam. Sending spam creates a negative marketing image. You may have experienced the frustration of being spammed.

Some of the advantages of email marketing are that it's low cost, it's quick, and with some basic tools you are able to track what happens with the emails (whether they are read, and whether those readers visited your website or made a purchase).

Opt-in is the key to successful newsletter marketing. If you don't have your own list yet, you can rent or lease a list from somebody else by advertising in their newsletter. Attributes of a successful newsletter: short, concise, and useful!

10.4 Affiliate marketing

This business model involves you using a company or person to promote your business products or drive prospects to your website. Affiliate marketers can generate a great deal of traffic.

For example, if you do not have an e-commerce shopping cart feature on your website, an affiliate marketing site could take orders for your company, and receive a commission of, say, 10 percent for each order processed.

An example of this would be a floral shop. If you type in keywords in a Google search, that you would like a florist in a particular city, you will find that most of the sites that show up are affiliate marketers' sites. The sites would have signed up florists in each city to assist in their marketing. For each order to the florist through the portal site, the florist would receive the order directly to fulfill through the portal site. A written agreement with the affiliate marketing site would set out the referral fee for each order.

Affiliates don't always process orders for you, they may just be referrers and send customers your way for a commission, whether it's a commission for each lead or for each sale. There are many different options for working with affiliate marketers.

10.5 Blogging

In this concept, you would have a section of your website (or a separate site completely) where you would publish regular messages from your company about your products. For example, you could talk about the benefits of your product, and have other reviewers discuss why they like your product, etc. A blog is more informal and informational in nature. Similar to an online diary, it is structured to create a positive business relationship and image with your existing or potential customer.

10.6 Social media marketing

Social media marketing can be immensely effective, and sometimes free or inexpensive to access. Social media sites have an incredible number of members or viewers in the many multiples of millions. You can place information about the benefits and usefulness of your products on these sites. For example, on YouTube, you could place a video showing how effective your product is. You would want to get expert advice on how to build keywords and text into your message in order to optimize the number of viewers.

Some of the most popular social networking sites include: Facebook, Twitter, LinkedIn, YouTube, Flickr, and MySpace. Be sure to check each one out — each has its merits and setbacks for marketing.

There are many other marketing options, including podcasting (similar to broadcasting, only online), and online forums to bring in viewers and prospective customers.

Speaking to an Internet consultant with experience and positive references would be a suggested first step. You need customized feedback on what type of Internet marketing plan would best meet your needs and budget.

11. Creating a Great Website

You are now ready to establish a website on the Internet. As mentioned earlier, to stay competitive, your website should be interactive and should allow the users to get information about your business and its products. Research shows that vendor reliability and the quality of information are major issues of concern for people dealing on the Internet.

Quality websites can be developed by using the following techniques.

11.1 Present a professional corporate image

Although these points apply to other traditional marketing methods, it is critical that you use them on the Internet.

(a) Provide a corporate profile that describes your business establishment. Develop visitor confidence in your business by describing the size of your business, the number of years you have been operating, and your association with other reliable companies.

(b) Provide news releases and articles to demonstrate the financial health of your business. Customers want to know that they will receive the products they order and that you will be around to provide after-sale service.

(c) Make sure the material you are providing is accurate and reliable. Check the facts, and do not forget you are dealing with a well-informed audience.

11.2 Establish the product benefits early

As in all advertising, you should identify your product's key benefits and introduce them early in your presentation. You want to invite the user to read on.

You should then elaborate on the key benefits and introduce other benefits. The Internet combines the advantages of visuals, text, ample white space, and possibly sound.

11.3 Anticipate customer questions

To gain the advantage of interaction you need to anticipate your customers' questions and offer some way to answer those questions. For example, in addition to providing answers to the most commonly asked questions, you could provide an email address for feedback and unique queries.

11.4 Create a dynamic message

Proper design and use of graphics, photos, and text will help make your message dynamic. You may want to consider giving visitors to your site the ability to enlarge the photos in the site or access more photos by clicking on certain icons.

One common problem of Internet advertisements is too much graphic content. Visitors to your site are likely not willing to wait a long time for pictures or graphics to download. You need to strike a balance between the desired number of graphics and the willingness of visitors to wait. Give visitors the ability to skip the graphics or get to relevant information during the download.

11.5 Create a domain name

One of the most important decisions you'll have to make regarding your Internet presence is your domain name. Unfortunately, most of the best names are already taken. Try a search on www.verisign.com, www.register.com, or www.cira.ca to see if the name you would like is already taken. At this point, most businesses that want a "generic" name will have to settle for multiple-word names, for example, www.buyfromusplease.com. If your business name has a truly unique spelling, you may find that it is still available, but be prepared to consider alternatives.

When deciding on the domain name and address to your website, use words that are easy to pronounce and, if possible, that describe your business or its products. The more memorable your address, the more visits you will have to your site, resulting in more sales.

11.5.a How to register a .com, .net, or .us name

You can register and pay for a "dot com" domain name, or several other variants such as ".org," ".net," or ".us" through www.verisign.com and www.register.com. The cost varies and is approximately $70 USD for two years, payable in advance. Thereafter, you'll pay $35 USD per year to maintain the name's registered status. These prices could change over time due to competitive reasons.

You need to provide some technical information to register a domain name, specifically, primary and secondary host-name and net address details. You'll also need to provide some contact information for an administrative contact/agent, technical contact (typically, the administrator of the website), and billing contact. If you do not have this information, your ISP can provide it or, for a fee, help process the registration.

11.5.b How to register a .ca domain name

In countries other than the United States, other domain suffixes are available, denoting the country of origin. In Canada, a company can register a ".ca" domain pursuant to some conditions: the company must be a legally registered business in the country, or the registrant must be a Canadian citizen. The Canadian Internet Registration Authority (CIRA) administers all domains that end with .ca. You can find out more about registering a .ca domain at www.cira.ca.

11.6 How to design an effective website

You only have a few seconds to catch a reader's eye so keep your web page short. A short list of your top attractions or newest products is better than a long list of everything under the sun. The following suggestions will help you build an effective website:

- *Short headlines and lists.* Keep headlines to six words or less. Keep lists to 10 items or less.

- *Make it interesting.* Involve the reader. A description of a product's benefits is always more effective than a list of its features. Remember, explain, don't just describe. Invite action and always avoid passive-tense phrases.

- *Great pictures.* In order to get quality pictures to illustrate your website, the web designer needs to have access to a scanner, and a good-quality original photograph or artwork. Don't use flyers or photocopies because they can produce an unpleasant grainy pattern when scanned.

- *The big picture.* Don't fall prey to "clip art syndrome," in which amateur designers litter their pages with several small images. In design work, the secret is to be bold. Make the design stand out and take command of the reader's attention.

- *Focus attention.* When designing a logo or headline, pick the most important word and emphasize it.

- *Simple typefaces.* Limit the use of exotic typefaces or, in the case of web pages, graphics that look like typefaces. If angled, warped, stretched, shadowed, or italicized text isn't essential to the message you are trying to convey, resist the urge. Never use an exotic typeface as body text (the lettering that comprises the "body" of your message). Don't use more than three or four typefaces in a single page. Never use all capitals in the body text; it's okay for short headlines but quickly becomes tiring to read in the body text.

- *Contrast is the key.* All emphasis is no emphasis. Contrast is the key to a successful design. As a general rule, use a bold or extra-bold sans serif typeface such as Arial, Helvetica, or Swiss for headlines, prices, and phone numbers. Most web designers now recommend sans serif typefaces for body text as well.

- *White space helps.* Don't crowd every inch of your page with text. Let the headlines breathe. It's especially important to leave plenty of white space as a border around your page.

- *Contrast is good.* If you are using tables (boxes), follow the rule of thumb about borders in the last tip. Don't crowd text in a box that's too small. When legibility, comprehension, and retention increase, your page's message is more effective.

11.7 Gathering customer information from the Internet

Are you trying to figure out how to make your Internet site pay? Do you wish you could read your customers' minds? Maybe you can. The Internet is gaining popularity as a source of online information. Buyers are increasingly using the web to shop for and compare products.

Gathering and making sense of the behavior of visitors to your website will help you focus your online services to better meet their needs. Trading patterns can reveal something of how people shop, what they are interested in, and what they are thinking about. This will also help you in your advertising efforts.

11.7.a Tracking number of visitors and page popularity of your site

Online usage logs are a standard or optional feature of virtually every web server. For example, one of the many features added to Microsoft's Internet Information Server is the ability to log hits to the web server and access these logs remotely. In the absence of the more sophisticated tools listed below, this information can help you determine where a visit originated from, its time and duration, and, of course, what the visitors came to see.

Typically, these logs record every page view and every visitor to the site. There are inexpensive programs that provide charts, summaries, and other facts that can help you make sense of the usage patterns at your website. Some hosting companies automatically include "traffic stats" on customer use of your website for your tracking and marketing purposes.

Obviously, the reading pattern of online visitors to any particular website doesn't tell the whole story. There is much to be said for asking visitors outright how they feel about the service and products they obtain from you. Find out what products they are thinking of purchasing in the coming months, and what part of your operations could be improved upon. People like to know you care about their opinion.

No matter what trend-analysis solutions you favor, a tool that allows you to examine the most popular items and figure out the patterns is a valuable addition to your Internet business strategy.

11.7.b Using "cookies"

It is possible, with custom-coded web pages, or commercial offerings from a number of vendors, to gather persistent data known as a "cookie" when a visitor arrives at your website. These cookies can tell you if a user has been to the site before. Some sites can and do collect other information without your knowledge when you visit their site. Thus, many users are rightfully concerned about cookies that are secretly collected while they browse the web. You cannot obtain a user's email address with a cookie. If obtaining a visitor's email address is your goal, you'll have to entice them to leave it, possibly in exchange for access to a subscribers-only area, or by providing something else of value.

11.7.c Email

One of the key ways Internet contacts can be established is, of course, via electronic mail. Email has emerged as the number one method of customer-vendor contact and many suppliers are practically drowning under the ever-increasing tide of email.

The real likelihood is that, sooner or later, you are going to need to improve your ability to efficiently respond to emailed information requests. As your company's Internet presence grows, you are going to receive a lot of email, so you had better have a plan in place to deal with this. Some of the methods you may find useful for managing requests for information include having "bots" which is an email form letter that automatically provides information on certain topics. You, or your email service provider, could set up a bot to automatically email a price list or a product specification sheet in response to a request. For maximum efficiency, provide several email addresses on your website, in which visitors can categorize their response, for example, the relation to sales, information, technical help, or a problem with the website.

You can use a bot to thank people for writing and to let them know that their letter has been received and that it will be read. Remember, however, that a bot is no substitute for a personal reply. Although the bot provides an immediate response to let people know their message made it through and that it is appreciated, such missives ring hollow unless you follow up with a personalized human reply.

12. Legal Issues

Before setting up business on the Internet, you need to address non-marketing issues such as legal issues. Generally, the law applies to the Internet environment as it applies to the non-Internet world. Commercial tax, contract law, copyright, freedom of speech, censorship, and the right to privacy, as well as criminal law and pornography laws, apply to the Internet. It is good business to also be familiar with the laws of other countries so that your operation may be consistent with their laws, while respecting their cultural norms. Chapter 18 covers general legal issues relating to product liability. See also *Cyberlaw Canada*, another book published by Self-Counsel Press.

13. Conclusion

Information is a key competitive advantage in today's business environment. As we enter the information superhighway, we can expect greater use of video conferencing, distance learning applications, and interactive exchange. The development of new technology and applications will attract new entrants as well as new marketing opportunities for many entrepreneurs.

13
THE COMPETITIVE EDGE

Today's consumers have high expectations. The educated tastes of the 1980s have created a new set of consumer demands that are here to stay.

Consumers responded to the recession in the early 1990s by repaying debt, deferring large purchases, and cutting down on nonessential goods and services. Recovery is slow, and the recession has changed people's buying habits.

Consumers are more prudent and are managing their consumption more carefully. Nowadays, cars such as Infiniti and Lexus are in vogue because they emphasize quality and value. Consumption of luxury goods is reduced; now people are more selective. The lesson of the 1990s is that people don't want to lower their standard of living, they just want to pay less for it.

Enhanced technology has given rise to a proliferation of new products. In 1980, a consumer could find 13,000 items in a supermarket. In 1990, close to 30,000 items could be found on the same shelves.

Factors such as continual introduction of new products, escalation in technology, changing family composition, and new competitive and economic realities are influencing consumer buying habits. The need to match your product benefits with consumers' specific needs has become more important.

The customer defines quality, not the manufacturer. Today, lifestyle often determines product choice, while price acts as a restraint. If you know what your customers want and what influences them, you've got the competitive edge.

1. Type of Competition

From an economist's point of view, there are five different types of competition. Depending on the type of product you provide, you must consider more than whether another company offers a similar product and service to the same type of customer.

1.1 Monopoly (one firm)

A pure monopoly is only one firm providing a product or service. In many countries, the postal service or utility companies represent a typical monopoly. With little or no competition, such firms may charge a high price with little advertising and a minimum amount of service. In most countries, monopolies are regulated.

Competition in monopolies is concerned with maintaining the public interest and maintaining a reliable service at a reasonable price. This prevents negative public reactions that could lead to political interference or deregulation.

A partial monopoly exists when a firm gains an advantage through a patent, license, or economy of scale. For example, sales of suntan lotion have increased due to concern about harmful radiation. As a result of the high demand for safe suntan lotion, the company that makes the patented chemical Parsol 1789 has been able to secure a price advantage because their products block ultraviolet "A" and ultraviolet "B" rays, which are said to contribute to premature aging and skin cancer. In such a situation, the first company to come out with the product gains a competitive advantage.

1.2 Oligopoly (few firms, same product)

Oligopolies are a few firms that provide essentially the same product (oil, steel, etc.) at the same price. Such industries compete in service and mode of distribution.

1.3 Differentiated oligopoly (few firms, similar product)

A differentiated oligopoly consists of a few companies making products that are fairly similar such as automobiles or cameras. In such industries, competition comes from different product features, styles, and services provided.

1.4 Monopolistic competition (many firms, different products)

Monopolistic competition is many firms offering different products such as furniture, shoes, and clothing. In monopolistic competition, firms compete by providing different products to different markets.

1.5 Pure competition (many firms, similar products)

Pure competition consists of many companies offering similar products such as food or beverages. Pure competition differs from an oligopoly in that many firms offer the same product. In such industries, competition is focused on creating psychological differences, mainly through advertising. Where differences are difficult to achieve, firms have to compete by lowering their cost of production and distribution.

In a pure competitive environment where you are selling similar products, efficient production, a unique advertising theme, and a low price become very important. In a monopolistic competition, your ability to innovate and provide different products becomes your key competitive advantage. In a differentiated oligopoly, your product features, styling, and the ability of your front-line personnel to provide value-added services gives you a competitive edge. It is important to realize that how you compete is influenced by the type of product you sell.

2. Gaining the Competitive Edge

To compete, you must excel in at least one area. Your company philosophy, the market you cater to, and the type of product you provide will determine what area you should focus on. There are three main areas that can give you a competitive edge.

2.1 Operational efficiency

Operational efficiency means that you provide your customer with reliable products at a competitive price. Companies such as General Electric and Wal-Mart provide customers with quality goods and make these goods available when and where customers want them with minimal inconvenience at a competitive price. These companies are trustworthy and consistent in the delivery of their product.

Here is a list of factors you should consider to improve your operational efficiency.

(a) Connect all your business activities to real customer needs. Operational efficiency requires that you first identify the needs of your customer and align all your activities to ensure customer satisfaction.

(b) Reduce or eliminate activities and costs not related to serving customer needs. Reducing costs does not necessarily mean cutting your labor force or salaries, although at some time this may be necessary. Reducing costs may imply investing in state-of-the-art technology to produce more efficiently. It may mean re-engineering your delivery process and automating your inventory control and billing system to reduce time and cost.

(c) Create cross-functional responsibilities where everyone is responsible for customer service. Financial and manufacturing managers may need to work with the marketing manager to see how they can simplify and lower the distribution cost, while maintaining the same product quality and customer service. Site sales representatives may team up with technical maintenance personnel to provide better service.

(d) Integrate your company with good suppliers, distributors, and vendors, to enhance cost efficiency and smooth out the transfer of goods to the customer.

Operational efficiency requires that you outperform your competitor in the following areas:

- Respond quickly and adapt to market demands

- Provide a reliable and consistent product to satisfy your customer

- Produce and deliver your product at a competitive price

Operational efficiency focuses on efficient production and distribution capabilities and customer satisfaction.

2.2 Customer service

Kraft Foods and Home Depot's competitive strategy is to continually tailor their products to individual needs. For example, Home Depot's service philosophy is to "treat every customer like you would treat your mother, your father, your sister, or your brother." Home Depot clerks are expected to take the time necessary to solve a customer home-repair problem. Customer service-oriented companies do not compete on price, but on their ability to cater to individual needs and provide customized service.

The following is a list of factors to help you improve your customer service competitive strategy.

(a) Be flexible in producing and delivering your products and services. For example, Kraft Foods can deliver different product assortments to the different types of shopping groups that buy at each of their different stores.

(b) Train your employees to provide recommendations and give them the authority to satisfy customers' needs. Encourage employees to build long-term relationships with their customers.

(c) Provide an information system that educates employees and collects, integrates, and analyzes information on the customer. Home Depot employees' close attention to customer satisfaction provides timely and valuable information on customer needs.

(d) Customize a promotional program that provides relevant information to the right customer.

Customer service requires that you outperform your competition on the following:

• Fit your product to individual needs

• Provide customized service

• Provide relevant information and service to each group of customers

2.3 Product leadership

Product leadership means seeking to produce state-of-the-art products and services. Nike and Johnson & Johnson are examples of companies that lead in technology, bringing the latest in product design to the consumer. While technology and novelty are very important in product leadership, innovation comes from specific cues from the marketplace. In the mid-1980s, Nike lost dominance in the athletic shoe industry. Nike's founders understood the needs of athletes. After Nike started to lose sales, they decided to look at what other recreational products consumers wanted from an athletic shoe, such as a shoe for the weekend jogger or the recreational tennis player.

Nike regained its market share once they started to provide different athletic shoes for the different athletic needs of shoe users. As Nike officials have said, "While technology is still important, the consumer has to lead innovation."

But don't confuse innovation with variety. Too much variety makes all products look similar and you are forced to compete on price alone.

Here is a list of factors to help you improve your product leadership.

(a) Open communication with the consumer. Managers, design engineers, and production personnel must talk with the customers and dealers and observe how the product is used. Use focus groups and other research tools to supplement your observations.

(b) Foster a creative entrepreneurial environment. Encourage employees to bring forward ideas, however unconventional.

(c) Commercialize quickly on ideas. Product leaders must avoid bureaucracy and be ready to make a wrong decision rather than a late one or no decision at all.

(d) Product leaders should be their own best competitor; continually look for ways to improve your product.

Product leadership requires that you outperform your competition on the following:

• Maintain technology leadership in the eye of your customers.

• Provide enhanced benefits through improvement. The new product must be perceived to have a clear difference or advantage over the previous product, be aligned with the customer values, and easily understood and tested by the customer.

• Commercialize your idea quickly.

3. Choosing a Competitive Edge

What a consumer buys depends on his or her individual values. A consumer who wants a convenient, quality product at a cheap price shops at a discount store or a warehouse. If you are selling from a well-furbished retail store, the consumer may not believe they can get the best price.

Customers who want specific needs satisfied are not willing to make sacrifices. Some customers seek the latest or most unusual product. These customers like to be first and want only the best or latest of what technology offers.

The strategy you choose depends on what your market demands, the product you sell, and your company's values, resources, and expertise. Choosing the appropriate strategy will help you gain an edge over your competitor by better meeting your customers' needs.

4. Assessing Your Competition

It is possible to spend too much time and energy assessing your competitor at the expense of your customers. However, the cost of not knowing your competitor at all can be high.

Before you position yourself, you need to know something about your competitors. Worksheet 1 can help you evaluate your company against the competition.

In sports, it is important to have a good defense and a good offense; you only win when you score. In business, you score when you serve your customer. It is important to keep track of what your competitors do. However, too much attention paid to the competition may keep you from scoring.

For example, if company A notices that company B lowers its price, then company A may react by lowering its price. If company B increases its advertising, company A may react by increasing its advertising.

Lowering prices may attract customers who are bargain hunters and who won't be loyal once the sales promotion is over. Instead of following your competitor's lead in attracting the same customer, you could try to attract a customer who instead may prefer, for example, additional service.

The three competitive approaches discussed in section **2.** form a strategic framework to evaluate your competitive strategy. In a dynamic, changing environment, a framework can provide a pattern or approach to positioning. Although you need to continually monitor your operation to fit changes in the competitive environment, the companies that thrive are the ones that provide the most value to the customer.

While it is important to keep an eye on your competitor, the best way to compete is to do the following:

• Focus on your customers' needs.

• Stick to what you do best.

• Provide better value than your competitor.

WORKSHEET 1
ASSESSING THE COMPETITION

Evaluating Your Company Against Your Competitor

To evaluate your company against your competitor, you need to answer four important questions:

1. How would you describe your customer?

   _____

   _____

2. How would you describe your competitor's customer?

   _____

   _____

3. Why would a customer buy from you? Not buy from you?

   _____

   _____

4. Why would a customer buy from your competitor? Not buy from your competitor?

   _____

   _____

The following are provided to help you answer questions 3 and 4.

Describe your product benefits and weaknesses.

_____

_____

Describe your major competitor's product benefits and weaknesses.

_____

_____

Describe how your customer sees your product benefits in terms of quality level, style, options, packaging, etc.

_____

_____

Describe how your competitor's customer sees —

    (a) your product

    _____

    _____

    (b) your competitor's product

    _____

    _____

Describe the advantages and disadvantages of your company and your competitor in terms of distribution and outlet location.

    (a) Your company

    _____

    _____

    (b) Your competitor

    _____

    _____

5. Describe your company's promotion capability in terms of advertising and media used, publicity, and special promotions.

    _____

    _____

6. How does your competitor differ in its promotion capability?

    _____

    _____

7. Describe the needed service and complimentary service you provide with your product. Who provides the service? (e.g., your sales staff, technical personnel, etc.)

    _____

    _____

8. How is your service different from your competitor?

   _____

   _____

9. In relation to your company, what are your competitor's —
   Sales?

   _____

   Market share?

   _____

   Profit margin?

   _____

   Investment?

   _____

   Production capacity?

   _____

10. Describe the critical factors that could upset your competitive advantages.

    _____

    _____

11. Could an advantage be gained from a change in —
    Financial strength?

    _____

    Technology?

    _____

    Economies of scale?

    _____

12. Describe how your competitor is likely to react to a competitive change. Is it likely to:

    Do nothing? ☐   Lower its price? ☐

    Change its product? ☐   Change its promotion? ☐

13. Describe your major competitor's strengths and weaknesses.
    Competitor's strengths

    _____

    _____

    Competitor's weaknesses

    _____

    _____

14. Describe your company's strengths and weaknesses.
    Your strengths

    _____

    _____

    Your weaknesses

    _____

    _____

15. Based on your company's strengths and market opportunity, describe how you
    will differentiate yourself from your competitor.

    _____

    _____

14
MANAGING IN A COMPETITIVE WORLD

In today's competitive environment, the way you manage your work force can be your most important competitive edge. One dissatisfied customer can cost the profits of five satisfied customers. While close to 14 percent of customers switch to competing brands because of dissatisfaction with the product, 68 percent of customers switch due to indifference shown by an employee serving them. If you don't treat your own people well, they won't treat other people well.

1. What Happened in the Past

Before the industrial age, goods were produced by individual crafters. In the industrial age, goods produced by individual crafters were replaced by groups of companies and a die system. Those with access to capital and a good record keeping management style could do well.

In 1909, a Model T car cost $950. After Ford introduced the mass production process, the cost of the Model T went down to $360. The mass production process replaced the industrial age die system (which is like a cookie cutter system developed when the first concept of mass production started), giving rise to economies of scale and making cars affordable to the masses. The scientific management style was born. The new successful manager was the one who brought in specialization and standardization of production. Product output exploded, and for the first time, people enjoyed products previously not available to the masses.

Craftsmen provided personalized service to their customers. The industrial age, followed by mass production, put distance between the worker and the customer. However, for many years that distance was not a problem because most products were serving a growth market with similar consumer needs. What was important was to make the product affordable and available.

2. What Changed

The surge in technology, the proliferation of new products, increased affluence, and changing family composition has changed the needs and characteristics of the marketplace. The similarity between products, more choices, and competition for market attention has created a high level of market fragmentation.

Today, you need to fine-tune your total marketing offer to customers' distinctive requirements. We have entered the information age, and although economy of scale is still important, it needs to be supplemented with economy of knowledge. Computers are the tools of the information age; however, knowledge resides with your employees. They must be trained to apply and deliver it.

The management style that emerged from the mass production era was well-suited to companies then. Today's management style must suit the information age and the return of employee contact with the customer.

Management style, in large part, needs to conform to what the customer expects. When people visit McDonald's for a hamburger, they expect food served quickly. Individual service such as extra onions or tomatoes would slow down the service and annoy waiting customers. However, when you go to Home Depot with a home repair problem, you expect the staff to take the time to solve your problem and sell you only those products you need. The operational efficiency of McDonald's requires a different management approach from Home Depot's individual customer approach.

The most important marketing decision you can make is to cater to your customers' needs. That in turn imposes your management style. Just as a good sailor understands how to adjust sails to suit the wind, so a good manager adapts management style to fit the situation.

3. The Importance of Frame of Mind

Competitiveness is a combination of a company's resources and its management goals. Too often, attention is paid only to external factors to explain sales declines — that type of thinking is a problem.

Management's frame of mind is formed largely by education, relationship with peers, and, most of all, by experience. Managers' willingness to challenge their attitudes and to question old ways of doing things can be your best competitive edge.

4. Management Style

In today's environment, you need both a mix of leadership and effective management style. Leadership seeks opportunities; management solves problems.

If leadership is to provide the map, then management must do the driving. Sample 4 compares managers and leaders and their business strategies.

Leaders favor innovative solutions to problems and take risks. Leaders work well in flat, organic organizations that encourage individual participation.

Managers favor control and proven means to problem solving and decision making. The manager's rational approach favors traditional mechanical organizations that encourage uniform and reliable work.

LEADERS VERSUS MANAGERS: APPROACHES TO STRATEGY

Leaders	Managers
Leaders are more interested in the big picture and the impact of the decision.	Managers are more interested in details and how decisions are made.
Leaders encourage risk-taking and learning from mistakes. When "it ain't broke" may be the only time you can fix it.	Managers minimize risk and seek compromise between conflicting points of view. "If it ain't broke, don't fix it."
Leaders' authority derives more from interpersonal influence, shared goals, and the ability to shape ideas into action. Rewards are given for results.	Managers' authority derives from their position in the company hierarchy, the role each plays in the decision-making process. Managers are concerned with a balance of power. Reward is based on what is fair.
Leaders prefer a fresh approach to problems.	Managers prefer a logical approach with proven methods.
Leaders delegate extensively and promote two-way communication.	Managers delegate within limits and seek the right balance of communication.
Leaders are mainly concerned with achievement.	Managers are more concerned with a mix of achievement and control.
Leaders' strategies are more a product of the mind. Leaders have a high tolerance for chaos and uncertainty. Leaders seek to understand customers' needs through anomalies and emotional signals.	Managers' strategies derive more from spreadsheets. Analytical, persistent, and practical work is done to determine customers' needs and company direction.
Leaders are driven by outward circumstances and act according to conditions.	Managers are driven by inward circumstances and in accordance with company standards.
Leaders' organizations are more flat and organic.	Managers' organizations are traditional and structured.
Leaders form strong relationships in more intuitive and empathetic ways. A leader's sense of identity is not related as much to the organization as to self-reliance and achievement.	Managers form moderate and a wide variety of attachments. A manager's self-worth is highly related to the company and the role and duties for which he or she is responsible.

Most people have both leadership and managerial capabilities. To have either is neither good nor bad; both are a means to improved performance. In any organization, some individuals have a higher number of leadership characteristics, while others do better with managerial skills. This gives rise to the variety of management styles within an organization. The best management style is one that capitalizes on market needs.

5. How Does It Work?

Most businesses succeed as a result of the combined efforts of each member of the company working in teams or groups. Although both approaches require a mix of functional specialists, leaders are better suited to working with a team, while managers are best suited working with groups. Sample 5 compares working groups to teams.

The working groups carry out day-to-day activities. Teams enhance and complement an existing organization working group. The introduction of a new product, the rationalization of suppliers, or a new approach to customer service all lend themselves to a team approach. The type of team and how often it is used depends on the market you are serving and how you decide to compete. Both team and working group approaches require a customized mix of leadership and management skills.

6. Management Process

Managing is much more than just making decisions and supervising people. There are several elements that are important to effective management. They include path finding, making decisions, and executing your strategy. Each of these elements requires a mix of both managerial and leadership skills.

In deciding which type of management style is most suitable, you must consider the type of business and the competitive environment you are in, the market you cater to, your company's values, and your own personality.

6.1 Flexibility

For small- to mid-sized companies, it may not always be practical to form teams because you need everybody on board to do the day-to-day jobs. Managers must be flexible in adopting a leadership or managing approach in order to foster the appropriate team or work group environment.

6.2 Management fads

Over the years, many seminars have made promises with their guaranteed management formulas on how to better motivate your work force and increase productivity. Management by objectives, broadbanding, and total quality management have all been applied and overhauled at one time or another. Broadbanding, for example, allows workers to do more tasks by lumping together many jobs into one description, and eliminates multiple salary levels to encourage lateral movement among jobs. After its implementation, many employees complained about the lack of clear promotion. In many companies with poor morale, the desired result has not been attained.

There are management formulas that get results. However, no formula can fit all circumstances.

7. Adaptive Management

Trying to fit one management formula to all marketing environments nets poor results. Competition requires that your company positions

WORKING GROUPS VERSUS TEAMS: HOW THEY FUNCTION WITHIN A COMPANY

Working Groups	Teams
Goals, purpose, and the group are decided by upper management.	Goals and purposes are shaped by the team in response to management directives. Each member can take turns in leading the team.
The end product is a result of individual performance.	The end product is a result of combined individual efforts.
Meetings, discussions, and information exchange help individuals do a better job and align themselves with broader company objectives.	Meetings, discussions, and information exchange help promote the performance of the team and align each member with the project's specific objectives.
The performance objective is to promote efficiency and performance.	The performance objective is to solve a specific problem (e.g., reduce product defects by 25 percent).
A group is usually composed of members from various departments within the company.	A team's composition should include complementary technical and functional expertise mixed in with members who have decision-making and interpersonal skills.
Goals are related to a prioritized agenda and implemented by specific individuals within the hierarchy of the organization.	Goals should be compelling, motivating, and attainable. For example, to be the first to introduce a given product.

itself as operationally effient, provides a high level of service, or becomes the first with a new product. Your company's competitive orientation requires that you adapt your management style accordingly.

Management must constantly ask the questions that tie the needs of the consumers to the action of the company. For example, a technological breakthrough or innovation is not necessarily what a customer wants. Customers seek new products that can provide a solution to their problem or that say something about who they are. In order to discover what the customer seeks, it is important that the research and development people, the designer, and the manufacturing staff work with the marketing team to find solutions for the customer.

Your key competitive strategy is to match consumer needs with product benefits and to gain advantage over your competition. Strategic vision requires that you identify areas of growth, select suitable products for your market, and establish constructive alliances with other corporations.

However, a vision can only be implemented through your work force. Your management style has a big influence on providing the synergy that's required to gain a competitive edge.

Your organization's structure and management style should provide the following competitive advantages:

(a) *Environmental scanning:* An information system that provides the latest on customer trends, changing legislation, new technology, competition, and relations with your supplier.

(b) *Organizational flexibility:* The organization must be flexible to adapt to changing market conditions.

(c) *Functional integration:* Specialized functions must learn to work together toward a common goal satisfying the customer.

(d) *Strategic alliances:* Form strategic alliances between independent corporations to provide access to changing technology and markets.

8. Managing Duality

Management needs to provide organizational structure and resources, and at the same time give employees the flexibility that promotes creative solutions. Structure needs to provide direction without preventing individuality. People want to do their own thing and still be part of something bigger. Managing is the ability to balance that duality.

Employees are no longer willing to salute. Most employees want a voice in their job and to feel they are contributing to a company's ability to operate. Every day your employees come into contact with customers to solve their problems. A company that listens to its employees and acts on their suggestions gains a competitive edge and enhances employee morale and motivation.

Where does your company stand on management and leadership? The questions on the following pages can help you analyze your needs.

1. What incentives and reward systems does your company use that reinforce a customer service-oriented approach?

    _____
    _____
    _____
    _____
    _____
    _____
    _____

2. Do all employees follow up and listen to the customer requests?

    _____
    _____
    _____
    _____
    _____
    _____
    _____
    _____

3. Does your management style encourage communication and initiative among the different levels and functional groups within your organization?

    _____
    _____
    _____
    _____
    _____
    _____

4. Do you share work, information, blame, and satisfaction?

    _____
    _____
    _____
    _____
    _____
    _____

5. Do you provide the necessary training and resources for employees to make decisions?

_____
_____
_____
_____
_____
_____
_____

6. Do employees make promises to customers they can keep? Do employees have enough authority to serve customers properly?

_____
_____
_____
_____
_____
_____
_____

7. Do employees deliver the goods to customers and meet your company standards?

_____
_____
_____
_____
_____
_____
_____

8. Do customers find it easy to do business with you? Are employees easy to contact and effective in relaying information?

_____
_____
_____
_____
_____
_____
_____

15
SELLING AS A MARKETING TECHNIQUE

Selling is an integral part of your marketing strategy. But the aggressive and sometimes questionable practices of used-car sellers and door-to-door peddlers and hucksters have established an unfortunate stereotype of salespeople. However, it needn't be that way. In professional sales, you don't try to sell the customer; rather, you try to help solve a problem by presenting both the advantages and limitations of your products. Professional selling involves understanding the prospective customer's needs and problems and offering a solution.

Compared to advertising or promoting, personal selling is flexible; salespeople can tailor their presentations to the customer based on customer feedback. While advertising triggers a desire, it is personal selling that more often brings actual sales.

The main limitation of personal selling is its high cost. Sales operating expenses can vary from 8 to 15 percent of net sales, while advertising, on average, varies from one to three percent of net sales.

1. Organization

You need a well-organized, focused selling program to accomplish your marketing objectives, not just a verbal presentation by your sales force. Everyone involved in your business participates in the selling program. How your staff communicates, their personal appearance, the office atmosphere, and the reception area, for example, are all critical to your marketing and selling programs.

1.1 Office location

Your outlet should be located where it is convenient to the customer. If you are dealing with businesspeople, they are comfortable in the downtown area. If you cater to middle-class families, a suburban location is best. The location should be consistent with the customer's self-image.

1.2 Reception

All your staff should be presentable, whether they deal up front with accounts or are involved behind the scenes. They should be able to speak in a pleasant and capable manner. Service or referral should be prompt. Avoid connecting customers to the wrong extension or putting them on hold.

1.3 Layout and decor

Interior design and decor conveys cues to your customers. Using the appropriate furniture and style, you can complement or cater to your customers' self-concepts. Details such as plants, lighting, color, seating, and spatial arrangements all need to be integrated to convey an image consistent with your company goals.

1.4 Dress code

A few seconds after meeting your employees, potential customers confidently form judgments about your business. Although first impressions can be wrong, they often persist even in the face of contrary evidence. Clothing is an important source of information during this process. Generally speaking, wear clean, quality clothing that fits properly. When in doubt, make the conservative choice.

2. Who Should You Hire to Sell?

Your sales force may be your major contact with the outside world. Consequently, opinions about your product or company are formed based on the impressions they make.

Often your salespeople might work long hours alone and are under mental and physical stresses rarely required by other jobs. Despite these demands, your sales force must be highly motivated, self-confident, persistent, and socially skilled.

Your sales force's selling style should vary according to the customer's personality. Some customers like to get to know the salesperson before they talk about the product. Others have little interest in who the salesperson is and just want to talk business. Try to find people who can sell the image of the company while adapting to the variety of customer personalities.

3. Persuasion

If you want to persuade someone of something, listening is more important than talking. One of the key elements in persuasion is sincere attentiveness to your customer's problem. Here are a few tips.

- Clear your mind. People often assume that their own feelings, needs and problems are similar to those of others.

- Show respect and tolerance for differences.

- Avoid value judgments and try to understand the customer's point of view.

- Focus on content. Don't concentrate on omissions.

- Be attentive to both the verbal and nonverbal messages.

- Be aware of your own influence. Don't misguide the conversation by concentrating your attention on selective issues.

- Review material related to the customer's problem. This allows you to ask pertinent questions.

- Don't get sidetracked.

- Don't get personal or be offensive or defensive.

- Let the customer know you understand. Summarize the points he or she makes.

- Be yourself. Canned approaches don't work in a professional setting.

4. Making Contact

Follow these steps to increase your leads:

- Ask satisfied customers to refer people to you.

- Ask staff to be alert for opportunities to provide your products.

- Join clubs or associations where you will meet or acquire contacts for potential customers.

- Check the news to uncover opportunities for new business.

- Check publications for leads.

- Find the published lists of building permits issued.

- Cold call.

- Use direct mail.

- Advertise.

- Enter trade shows.

- Draw up a mailing list from promotions and sales.

- Talk to salespeople who call on you.

After leads have been identified, they must be qualified, that is, you must make sure if and when they need your product.

5. How To Sell Effectively

5.1 Pre-approach

If you are dealing with a firm, research your prospect's business problems, interests, competitors, and market. Set up a meeting with the prospective client.

5.2 Appraisal

Use small talk to get to know each other, but listen carefully to what the prospective customer is saying. Take time to find out the customer's needs, concerns, and objectives.

Repeat and clarify what you perceive your customers require and be prepared to answer questions they are likely to ask.

Discuss your professional and technical competence. Be organized, well-groomed, and demonstrate that you have the ability to do the job well.

5.3 Presentation

The golden rule in making your presentation is to always display a sincere interest in the client's needs and situation. Demonstrate the use of the product, how it will benefit the customer, and how this is an improvement over what he or she is using now. Discuss the client's concerns and stress points of agreement.

Some firms require that you submit a proposal before your presentation. Others request a presentation first and then ask that a written proposal be submitted if they are interested. When writing a proposal, tailor it to the particular client. Be as concise and accurate as possible and resist the temptation to exaggerate product claims.

Demonstrate that you have the technical understanding to resolve the prospect's problems. Describe how you will approach the work scheduling, planning, etc. Include a biography of the senior staff and a summary of your firm's past experience. Remember, the quality of a proposal reveals your professional self-concept and the regard you have for your work.

5.4 Objections

Learning what objections you may routinely expect and how to handle them is crucial to your success. Welcome objections; they show interest on the part of the prospective customer and afford you an opportunity to close the sale. Clarify each objection by asking "Do you mean ... ?" Don't argue, EVER. You are two people on the same side of an issue trying to solve a problem. Ignore irrelevant objections. Question clients in such a way that they answer their own objections.

Present alternatives and try to discern which one the client favors. Briefly reiterate the favored proposal. Zero in on objections and try to resolve them. If objections are handled well, you can try to close the agreement.

5.5 Closing

The close is not clearly defined and may take one of several forms. Some successful salespeople simply take the order book out and start writing. The customer needs to be led into the buying decision by your skillful questioning and timely comments. Remember to take charge and simply ask for the order.

Selling sometimes requires negotiation. In such cases, it is important to use someone who is experienced in closing. The art of negotiation is covered in detail in specialized books you can find in libraries or bookstores.

5.6 Follow-up

Once the sale is made, it's not the end, it's just the beginning. Servicing the account is very important and may determine whether you get repeat business. Here are useful suggestions for following up your sales.

Stay in close personal touch with buyers. Take them to lunch or for coffee. Often buyers just seek reassurance that they made the right choice. Reap the benefits.

If necessary, educate the buyer on how to use his or her new product. Make sure the product operates properly so that your client remains satisfied with it.

Bring the client good ideas for his or her business. In other words, go out of your way to make sure an account is satisfied with the purchase.

6. How to Make the Sales Job Easier

Selling is easier and more rewarding if you're sure your product is needed by the market and if you have a well-organized, well-planned sales program. The sales manager should be capable of motivating the salespeople and training them in sales techniques. Train your staff to sell other new and different products to their present customers.

Encourage key individuals of the company to join service clubs, trade associations, and professional organizations. Most salespeople can be motivated by providing status and financial incentives. A golf club membership or bonus can be offered based on the number of leads provided, the number of dollars billed or the increase in business over last year. Combine entertainment with selling. Professionals could be given expense accounts to entertain prospective customers.

How effective are your employees at selling? The questions on the following pages can help you assess your sales force's abilities and the areas where they need more support.

1. In what ways does your staff provide you with effective feedback on customer opinion?

    _____

    _____

    _____

    _____

    _____

2. Are customers handled in a courteous, professional manner by all of your staff? Is your office staff well-groomed? Do they present the image you wish?

    _____

    _____

    _____

    _____

    _____

3. What fringe benefits do you offer your employees? How does this compare to the competition?

    _____

    _____

    _____

    _____

    _____

4. In what ways can you assess each salesperson's performance?

    _____

    _____

    _____

    _____

    _____

5. Is your operation evaluated on a regular basis? By whom? What steps are taken to remedy problems?

    _____

    _____

    _____

    _____

    _____

6. Have you identified your long-term requirements for human resources? What are they?

7. What is your plan for reviewing your employees for promotion, salary increases, bonuses, commissions? How do your employee wages compare with local wages for similar work? How do you retain competent employees?

8. Are your job descriptions, responsibilities, and degrees of authority clearly stated?

9. Would your employees benefit from training courses, seminars, and conferences? What criteria will you use for selection?

16
IMPLEMENTING THE MARKETING PLAN

1. Controlling Implementation

Your action plan puts your long-anticipated marketing program in place. But you must ensure the plan is executed. Establish a control system to see if the marketing plan is being accomplished on schedule.

Planning and implementing a control system tests the employees who perform each marketing task. You need powerful personal qualities, such as devotion, dedication, and faith, from them. But establishing controls assures the progress of your marketing plan; they control the work, not the people who do the work. Properly applied, controls can be an inspiration to those accomplishing the work, for controls provide clarity, direction, and feelings of achievement. And they test your ability to lead your employees toward accomplishing each goal. If you are a one-person business,

your control system will test your self-discipline and determination.

2. Setting a Schedule

Plan your control system using the deadlines of the marketing plan. In the action plan, identify dates on which you'll check back and complete assigned tasks. Using any technique that works for you, note those deadlines on your daily calendar, where you'll be sure to see them. Or, mark them on a full-fledged project chart, dating each task of each activity of each strategy. The chart reminds all team members of upcoming deadlines.

Whatever your system, remember to keep it simple. Fancy charts and complex staff reports don't create new business and detract energy from the real marketing task.

Note: This chapter is drawn entirely from *Marketing Your Service* by Jean Withers and Carol Vipperman, another title published by Self-Counsel Press.

Controls work best when some quantity — a date or number — is applied as a goal for the action plan. With the quantitative goal, everyone's expectations are clarified. Without it, no one knows for sure whether they have succeeded. Undoubtedly, some dates and numbers will change as implementation progresses, but having set them in the beginning moves your project into action. And when each quantitative goal is accomplished, confidence and enthusiasm grows.

3. Staying on Schedule

Two things have a great impact on achieving strategies on schedule. One is having a realistic time line for each independent strategy. Without giving up too much time or energy to each project, plan more conservative deadlines than you think necessary. A delay after long, careful planning may seem frustrating to the aggressive, results-oriented, and optimistic business owner. Recognize, however, that unrealistic deadlines can be demoralizing.

The second thing that will help you stay on schedule is having a time line for each strategy that meshes with the others. Be certain that any strategies to be accomplished simultaneously by the same personnel are complementary (e.g., research and promotion, rather than researching and selling). Make certain that the time lines follow marketing logic: You shouldn't, for example, develop a brochure when the target market is not yet decided.

4. Different Results Than Expected? Become an MD

When a control system is set in place, you'll know if the results you're getting are those you planned. For example, you might have planned to increase contact with existing customers by 10 percent, and now you are finding your staff is swamped and is making only about one-quarter of the contacts planned. Or, you anticipated attracting 10 percent new customers by the end of the year, and you've only acquired 1 percent and you have lost some existing customers.

Don't be tempted to give up, feeling that it's not working if you don't get fast results. It is better for the future of your business if, in the face of such frustration, you learn yet another marketing skill: that of Marketing Diagnostician (MD). Then, in the face of discrepancies in results, you'll be able to stop, think about your problem, and diagnose its causes.

Marketing diagnosis is less precise than medical diagnosis. As in medical diagnosis, the MD may not be able to answer every question; some results are simply beyond your control. Nevertheless, the process for diagnosing the reason for different results is clear. It starts with the step closest to implementation and, when necessary, works back to questioning the most fundamental decisions.

4.1 The diagnostic process

To diagnose an implementation problem, relieve yourself of the highly charged word problem. Approach it as a puzzle. Discuss the puzzle thoroughly in closed meetings with the people who actually do the work. Ask which parts of the marketing plan work and which don't. Recognize that, in times of confusion, people respond with varying degrees of honesty. Back up oral assessments of the puzzle by gathering its pieces, results, information, and memoranda.

Since you are wearing the hats of both the MD and the product marketer whose money is on the line, make a special effort to stay calm during diagnosis. Stress reduces the ability to take effective action. Give your creative self an opportunity to work on the puzzle by relegating it to your subconscious and trying to relax. Let your subconscious ponder what the fundamental issue is, not who is to blame for it. Look at what should be done differently rather than merely restating the problem.

Ultimately, ask yourself the following questions:

- Is the way you are implementing the strategy at fault? For example, did you rely too much on referrals from previous clients? Perhaps you should pursue referrals from other sources more actively as well.

- Did you make an error in the plan itself? For example, did you choose too many target groups which, in retrospect, could have been the wrong marketing strategy. Instead, you could focus on key target groups and serve them well.

- If the plan is sound, were the original objectives as set by management valid? For example, should you have set an objective of increasing market share by 20 percent in a new area? Perhaps you should increase market share within one target market by 30 percent and plan to introduce your products to a new market by the end of the year.

4.2 Getting well again

Once you identify the cause of the problem, cure it. Curing it may simply require changing the strategy or it may mean altering fundamental precepts on which decisions were made. In either instance, a change requires cooperation from all staff involved. Don't let foot dragging happen. Face the need for change honestly. Then lead! Court, cajole, encourage, and restate the new objective until you are accused of being a broken record. Assisting staff through such change is one of those management challenges from which you'll inevitably grow.

5. Common Pitfalls to Avoid When Marketing

Now that you have a better understanding of the factors involved in marketing, you should know about the common pitfalls to avoid. The following are some of the frequent sources of frustration and areas that create problems:

- Unclear understanding of market due to failure to prepare, update, and follow a marketing plan

- Unwillingness or inability to obtain, organize, and analyze marketing information

- Ignoring or being unaware of what customers actually need and want

- Developing a marketing approach based on the needs of the seller rather than the buyer

- Putting on sales promotions with terms and conditions based on product or business considerations rather than market criteria

- Being caught by surprise by changes in the market

- Relying too heavily on market research data instead of relying on or applying common sense

- Failing to implement and consistently maintain a customer feedback system, and failing to review the content of the feedback and make changes accordingly

- Having an inconsistent or inadequate sales coverage and market share across key market segments

- Relying on market data automatically without analyzing it or looking for the implications behind the data

- Lack of effective coordination with distribution channels
- Using an inefficient customer ordering system
- Inadequate training and compensation of sales force
- Forgetting that the customer is always right
- Failing to keep delivery promises
- Failing to quickly and effectively deal with customer complaints
- Pricing a major product too low and hoping that the volume will compensate for the discount
- Being rigid rather than creative in thought, thereby missing potential innovative solutions and opportunities
- Lack of repair service; shoddy workmanship on repairs
- Poor product quality; exaggerated product claims
- Unsuitable or poor packaging; inadequate labeling or instructions

Employees should be trained on matters dealing with customer satisfaction. Feedback should be elicited from employees on methods of improving the quality of service to customers.

6. Systematic Marketing Diagnosis

Although solving a single marketing problem requires considerable time, energy, and effort, ignore the temptation to forget the problem once it is corrected. Instead, remember that each strategy is related to others. Review other strategies and make the adjustments necessary to continue on the way to a successful marketing plan for your business.

As you implement your marketing plan, work through the marketing diagnosis questions that follow this chapter. The answers will help you work through your problem, that is, your puzzle.

QUESTIONS

1. Why do you think there is a problem?

_____

_____

_____

_____

_____

_____

_____

_____

_____

2. What investigations have you made to determine this?

_____

_____

_____

_____

_____

_____

3. What are the symptoms?

_____

_____

_____

_____

_____

_____

4. What results do you want instead? (Restate your objective.)

_____

_____

_____

_____

_____

_____

5. What strategy are you implementing now to get those results?

_____

_____

_____

_____

_____

_____

6. What is your assessment of that implementation to date?

_____

_____

_____

_____

_____

_____

_____

_____

7. Did you originally set the right objective?

_____

_____

_____

_____

_____

_____

_____

_____

8. What are the possibilities? What could you do instead?

_____

_____

_____

_____

_____

_____

_____

9. What corrective action should you take now?

_____

_____

_____

_____

_____

_____

_____

17
INTERNATIONAL MARKETING

In an increasingly interdependent world economy, you need to consider the advantages of moving into international markets. There are several reasons for the change to an international marketing era.

- Increased migration, consumer affluence, travel, and exposure to world products

- New economic powers, such as Japan

- Increased industrialization of developing countries

- Integrated financial markets and international financial services

- Decreased transportation costs and easier shipping

- Improved communication and increased technological change

- Liberalization of trade restrictions and favorable government policies

- Increased privatization of publicly owned corporations

- Growth of strategic alliances between companies and competitive interdependence

- Diminishing or saturated market size within one country

- Strategic company objective: Companies may want to compete internationally to gain economies of scale in manufacturing, to ensure source of materials, have access to new technology, increase their market exposure, and preempt competition

1. Going International

A vital part of international marketing is recognizing an unidentified need and satisfying it. When evaluating your prospects, consider the demographics and trends of that country and how you intend to position yourself against related industries and competitors.

The key to successful international marketing is understanding the international customer. It is easy to assume that because we share the same needs, we want to satisfy them in the same way. After all, we all have hopes and dreams for our kids to do well, the same concerns about crime, and the desire to have a home. It is exactly because we have so much in common that we make the error of thinking that we all want the same thing.

In North America, a greeting card with a verse is often sent to a friend to express a sentiment. Europeans, like North Americans, like to express their feelings too, but usually send a card without a verse, preferring to write their own greeting in a blank card. By nature, we are nearly alike; in practice, there are many variations in how we express our interest.

2. Assessing Your Global Market

Before you enter a foreign market, assess the profit potential and political risk in that country. Following are some factors you need to consider in evaluating market attractiveness.

2.1 Political environment

The political stability of a government is important to a business's long-term planning. A change in government could bring expropriation of your assets or put new demands on your business.

Some countries are very receptive to foreign firms while others make it difficult to enter.

Before Pepsi could compete in India, it had to promise to aid economic development in rural areas as well as provide the transfer of some technology. Germany does not allow use of soaps with phosphates. England has very strict regulations about information that can be given about a product in television commercials. Before you venture into a foreign country, you need to answer the following questions:

(a) How stable is the government? Would a change in government significantly alter how you do business? What are the chances that your property could be expropriated or your assets severely constrained?

(b) Will duties, taxation, or import quotas increase your cost?

(c) What government regulations must be satisfied (e.g., licensing procedures or customs handling)? What is the government's commitment to ownership or contractual obligations?

(d) Are there currency restrictions? Are you required to barter or offer buy-back arrangements?

(e) What are the profit remittance and exchange control requirements?

(f) How would a fluctuation in exchange rates affect your profit margin?

(g) Are there government programs that can assist you? What is the effect of administrative public procedure on your ability to operate?

(h) What effect do existing laws and regulations have on how you currently advertise or distribute your product?

(i) Are there interest groups that could jeopardize your business practices?

2.2 Economic considerations

The makeup of a country's economy is shaped by the output and the proportion of people who work in manufacturing, service industries, and agriculture. Other influences are total population, total income, and distribution of income among the population. Simple goods and services are consumed in countries where a large percentage of the population works in agriculture. At the other extreme, countries with a lot of industrial manufacturing and a large middle class are attractive markets for many different kinds of goods and services.

Developing countries represent a huge potential for goods such as food, clothing, and basic appliances. Companies that develop low-cost, high-protein foods could gain substantial advantages in such countries. Chile, a country with high natural resources, may represent a great opportunity for the export of tools and equipment.

When evaluating a country's economic potential, consider the following factors:

(a) The total population and its growth

(b) The number of people living in rural versus urban areas

(c) The gross national product (GNP) and income per capita

(d) The average household income

(e) Income distribution

Although economic factors can indicate areas of opportunity, they have to be interpreted with caution. GNP or income per capita should not be used in isolation. For example, Saudi Arabia and Portugal have a low income per capita, yet many people can afford luxury goods such as a Mercedes-Benz. If you based your decision just on income per capita, you may have decided not to export luxury cars. In such cases, income distribution is a better indicator of opportunity.

In countries such as China and India, bicycles are the main means of transportation, while in North America they are used primarily for recreation. Accordingly, money spent on bicycles as a percentage of the income per capita or by the number of people living in urban areas will be different. In both cases, decisions based only on GNP, income per capita, or the number of people living in urban areas, could result in missed opportunities for marketing suitable products to wealthy families or those with lower incomes.

In Europe, per capita spending varies from country to country. The British spend a higher percentage on restaurants, hotels, and home appliances but less on furniture and drinks. Germans spend a higher proportion on furniture, drinks, and vehicles but less on restaurants, hotels, and housing. The Italians spend more on food than on drinks.

When looking at economic factors, be careful not to lump all Europeans under one homogeneous consumer category. The same principle applies to other geographical areas such as Asia, the Far East, or North America. Economic factors can be very useful indicators of market potential when interpreted cautiously.

2.3 Cultural differences

Each country has its own set of values, rituals, customs, and taboos; its own culture. Edward Hall, a pioneer in cross-cultural studies, once said, "Interaction is the hub of the universe and everything grows from it." A large component of interaction is communication. For instance, Americans like to explore areas of difference, express personal differences, and arrive at conclusions when they discuss things. The Japanese avoid conflict in their discussions and look for areas of consensus. This difference has profound implications on how you negotiate contracts or advertise. For example, Americans use "hard sell" advertising that states clearly what the product benefits are, while the Japanese use "soft sell" advertising that suggests a mood and shies away from directly mentioning the benefits.

In international business, it is important to recognize other cultural values not as better or worse than yours, but as different. Adapt your management approach and marketing program to your host country.

3. Market Research

A global market strategy adapts products and services to each country. The ability to understand cultures, economic barriers, and potential political pitfalls requires a planned marketing research program.

The first step is to find information on population characteristics, economic variables, and consumer willingness to buy. Libraries, embassies, universities, the census bureau, and private marketing research agencies can be valuable sources of information. North Americans are used to having access to a well-balanced data bank with population demographics, consumer attitudes, purchasing behavior, and media usage. However, in foreign countries, complete data may not be available. In Europe, you may need to contact a variety of agencies in different countries to get data. You may have to rely more heavily on regional governments as well.

You are likely to encounter several problems doing research in a foreign country:

(a) *Language*. Although some countries have reports in English, many countries offer their reports only in their native language(s).

(b) *Methodology*. The procedure for collecting data and the treatment of data varies from country to country and among agencies. Although media ratings in northern Europe are similar to North America's, be cautious when comparing ratings from different countries.

(c) *Age of data*. Japan and Canada take a census every five years. The United States takes a census every ten years. Some countries rely on birth, death, and marriage certificates to determine the country's demographics.

(d) *Completeness*. Some countries, such as France and Germany, have strong concerns about privacy. With limited access to things such as voters' lists or names of apartment dwellers, it may not be possible to get pertinent information related to your marketing program. For example, Switzerland and Germany publish data on noncitizens. Canada collects data on religion. Neither of these topics are included in the US census.

The Japanese and Europeans believe that Americans are overly concerned with hard data. Before introducing the Toyota to North America, Japanese managers talked with Volkswagen owners about what they liked about small cars and what else they would like to see in a car. Japanese and European managers are more likely to use soft data, quantitative data, and a good dose of intuition to make decisions.

No amount of even the highest quality data can give you a complete picture of the situation. After you collect the hard data, it is important to visit the region to try to understand the local culture. Subtleties captured by intuition and supported by data can improve your decision making and mean the difference between failure and success.

4. Strategies for International Marketing

Companies that decide to compete in foreign markets must determine how to vary their marketing mix to suit local conditions.

At one extreme, you may decide to standardize your marketing offer in every country. Standardization offers economies of scale in production, ensures consistency in delivery, and saves time in advertising.

At the other extreme, you could customize your marketing mix to fit the local market. Standardization provides cost savings, while customization may provide a bigger market share.

In agricultural and resource economies, your best strategy is to make a product available and affordable. Standard products such as consumer electronics, appliances, or industrial goods may sell well in basic economies. In a manufacturing economy, deciding to standardize depends on your competitive strategy and how you decide to position yourself. Some standardization is important in companies that depend on operational efficiency or mass production. For others, as discussed in Chapter 13, innovation or customized service is more important depending on the customer group you decide to serve.

5. Product

There are several product strategies that you can follow in foreign markets.

5.1 Same product

Products such as machine tools, heavy equipment, automobiles, beer, wine and spirits, cameras, and consumer electronics (e.g., iPods, Levi's jeans, and Coke), have been sold successfully throughout the world. Selling the product unchanged offers strong economies of scale in manufacturing. Marlboro cigarettes have been sold worldwide with the same cowboy image. Levi's jeans are associated with an elite western style and Rolex watches with international prestige.

However, for most products, you need to alter your message to suit local customs. Pepsi's diet drinks in Europe are not as successful as in the United States. In some European countries and in Latin America, men consider low-calorie beverages effeminate. In these counties, Pepsi commercials show men engaged in "he-man" acts such as skydiving off a cliff and kayaking over a waterfall.

In a similar vein, the Japanese commute mainly by mass transit. For the Japanese, cars simply aren't as utilitarian as in North America; they are strictly leisure-time transportation. In Japan, car commercials need to stress the recreational aspects of the vehicle.

5.2 Product adaption

In Mexico, McDonald's uses chili sauce instead of ketchup on its hamburgers. Xerox engineered its 5100 copier so that it could be used both in the United States where heavier paper and dark ink is used, and in Japan where the preference is lighter weight paper and blue ink. A leading Italian shoe manufacturer had to make changes to its shoe to fit the thicker ankles and narrower, flatter feet of Americans.

You would think by producing one laundry detergent, you could sell it all over the world. Not so. Italian and Spanish men insist on an immaculate appearance and stain-free shirts. The German concerns about water pollution limit their use of phosphates. The Japanese were the first to adopt concentrated detergents in a smaller box with less packaging. Standardization of a product or advertising message is more practical under the following conditions:

- When there are similarities in culture, lifestyle, and purchasing behavior
- When there are similarities in economic characteristics and marketing infrastructures
- When competing against a similar competitor, as in your own country
- When selling industrial and high-tech products
- When selling elite and status products with international reputations

6. Promotion

Nuances in communication provide the richness that makes a message memorable. Communication is related closely to local taste. While the smell of apple pie can send North Americans for a second serving, it is the smell of curry that appeals to our Indian counterparts.

Colors and names have different meanings in different countries. In North America, brides dress in white; in Malaysia, brides dress in red. The name "Nova" for the Chevrolet car means "does not go" in Spanish.

Cultural and religious factors influence advertising. Islamic countries do not tolerate nudity or sexy advertising while Scandinavian countries do. In Saudi Arabia, women must be shown in a family setting. Advertising for children's products in Islamic countries needs to stress parental approval with less emphasis on children as decision makers. South Americans would not take kindly to showing men doing housework, while Canada and Sweden stress that sexism and sexual stereotypes should be avoided in advertising directed to children.

A country's regulations influence the type of advertising campaign. Although tobacco companies sponsor many sports events in North America, advertising cigarettes and tobacco is prohibited in many countries. In France, companies cannot use children to endorse a product. Germany prohibits any competing claims.

In addition to certain restrictions, there are subtleties that you need to consider. Compared to US television commercials, those in Britain tend to have less information and use a soft sell rather than a hard sell approach. British advertising attempts to entertain the viewer and create a mood, while US advertising generally provides more information. North American advertising is designed to make the product look better. In Japan, advertising is aimed at making the product look desirable. The Japanese are more likely to use evocative pictures that convey a mood and shy away from mentioning price or product features and quality.

Standardized advertising provides economies of scale in terms of development and production costs. Standardized advertisements may be successful where products provide the same benefits, are at the same stage of the product life cycle and usage, when the product name and packaging does not have to be changed, and where there is similarity in the competitive environment. However, for most products an advertising packaging that caters to local tastes is more effective.

Sales promotion, like advertising, is influenced by local flavors and government regulations. In the United States and Spain, coupons are the leading form of sales promotion. Coupons are frequently prohibited in Germany and Greece. The Germans and French prefer in-store price reduction. In Brazil, free gift wrap and extra products are preferred.

Although promotional similarities exist in many countries, these examples illustrate that sales promotions cannot be automatically standardized. Before you proceed, seek advice to ensure that your sales promotion is consistent with local regulations and accepted practices.

7. Price

Although pricing for international markets requires that you exercise the same discipline you would follow in your own country, in this section, we concentrate on factors that are particularly pertinent to international pricing. There are several factors that affect pricing for international markets.

7.1 Cost factors

As in your domestic market, you must determine your product cost. To your product cost, add additional packaging, shipping, export insurance, tariffs, agent's commissions, translated and promotional literature, and local distribution channel costs. These additional costs may make the price too high to survive in the export market. In Japan, for example, your final retail price may be greater because more intermediaries are required to get the product to the final consumer. However, these additional costs do not have to be taken as a given.

7.2 Marketing factors

The income level in the foreign country greatly influences the price you can charge. The price for necessities such as food or shelter is less critical in countries with high incomes. However, in countries with low incomes, people often produce their own food and shelter, so a high price almost guarantees people won't be able to afford it.

As in the domestic market, the type and number of competitors influences the price. If a product is new to the foreign market, you can charge a higher price. If you are introducing a known product, decide if you will charge the same, lower, or a higher price than the competition. See Chapter 6, section **4.**, on the product life cycle and Chapter 7 for a review of competitive pricing strategies.

A product can be perceived differently in different countries, necessitating a different price. In Spain, Levi's jeans cost more because they are viewed as a fashion item.

7.3 Economic factors

The general economic environment, inflation, foreign exchange, and government policy can influence or even determine your pricing decision. Foreign goods have become so central to the living standards of most nations that we have created a large interdependency between national economies. A change in economic conditions, government rules, or financial circumstances can greatly affect exchange rates.

When buying foreign goods or selling your goods in a foreign country, the process involves two purchases: the purchase of the foreign currency and the purchase of the goods. A decline in the domestic currency value makes your export product cheaper and more price competitive against a similar product produced in the foreign country. An increase in the domestic currency value may make exporting more difficult.

Similarly, the rate of inflation can influence the value of your offer. Rates of inflation vary from country to country and over time. When selling your goods in countries with very high inflation, payments received 30 days after the purchase are worth less than payments made on the day of purchase. Substantial discounts combined with large penalties may be required to encourage the customer to pay immediately.

In most countries, governments have rules and regulations that influence the price of products and services. The rules may apply to the entire spectrum of goods sold or be specific to some industries. For example, most countries have rules to prevent dumping to stop foreign companies from selling their products below cost. Before entering a foreign country, you need to determine if government policy or industrial reaction could hinder your pricing strategy.

8. Distribution

Once you decide to enter a country, you must determine what presence will produce the best opportunities. First, consider these two things:

(a) Whether to produce and export from your existing facilities or to produce in the foreign country

(b) The level of ownership to adopt in your export distribution and production facility

Following are several alternate strategies to use when entering a foreign country.

8.1 Exporting

Exporting means selling your domestic products to international markets. Both large and small firms can do very well in the export business. Here are some advantages and disadvantages of exporting.

Advantages

- Expanded markets from an increased number of customers

- Increased market base for firms where domestic sales face strong competition and oversaturation

- Potential for high demand when introducing a relatively new product to that market

- High demand when entering a market with low competition or serving a market niche not served by competitors

- Lower production cost from economies of scale

- Increased profits from lower unit cost and shared fixed cost with domestic sales

Disadvantages

- Additional and more complicated financing

- Higher credit risk

- Possible product modifications

- Additional cost in communication, travel, and training

- Additional staff

8.2 Indirect exporting

In indirect exporting, you sell your product to a go-between in your domestic market who contracts with foreign markets or buyers. Your primary role is to find good go-betweens to assist you in developing sales abroad. There are several types of go-betweens who can assist you in exporting; they vary from export brokers working on commission who bring foreign buyers and domestic sellers together, to export merchants and trading houses that purchase your products directly for export themselves.

Indirect exporting is suitable for companies with limited resources or with little or no experience in exporting. Indirect export is less risky and allows you to test the market with little commitment from your own resources. The go-betweens provide a knowledge of foreign markets and reduce your credit risk as well as expenditures on staff and advertising.

Disadvantages of indirect exporting include a lack of direct contact with the foreign buyers, little or no information on customer needs and preferences, sharing profits with the go-betweens, and contract terms that may limit your flexibility.

8.3 Direct exporting

In direct exporting, you deal directly with the foreign buyer or an intermediary located in the foreign markets. Direct exporting offers you a greater degree of control over the distribution of your products and flexibility to react to changing market conditions. With direct exporting you can decide on distribution channels, promotion, pricing, and required services. Direct export puts you in touch with the customer and can give you feedback on customer needs and preferences.

However, foreign distributors may have competing brands and often pay attention to the brand that offers the best profit margin. With increased sales volumes, or where your product requires special skills to sell, exporting to your own subsidiary may be more profitable. Operating your own subsidiary requires additional expenses that need to be measured against sales volume.

8.4 Licensing

Licensing means granting the rights to commercially exploit a patent or trademark to a foreign company for a fee or royalty. The foreign company gains a patent which protects a product, technology, production expertise, or trademark which protects a product name. You gain foreign distribution capabilities and presence without an equity investment.

Licensing agreements are subject to negotiation and so vary from company to company. There are several advantages and disadvantages to licensing as follows.

Advantages

- Saves capital in manufacturing operations, which is critical if the market potential of the target country is small

- Allows management to devote resources to core issues

- Avoids potential risk in countries with uncertain political and economic situations

- Is the only means of entry to countries that prohibit free import of products or where government favors building local industry

Disadvantages

- Dependence on foreign company to produce revenues

- Uncertainty ensuring expected product quality standards

- Possibility of foreign company turning into a competitor after the license expires

- Pursue licensing when revenue from other forms of entry would be less than licensing

8.5 Franchising

Franchising, similar to licensing, is a contractual agreement between your company and a foreign company to use your brand name, logo, products, and mode of operation. McDonald's and Burger King are examples of successful franchises. Franchising is popular in the fast food industry, real estate, and the car rental business. It also lends itself to many other types of small businesses where standardization of products and systems can be maintained. Franchising works best for a unique product or service with operational and management systems that can be easily duplicated.

8.6 Manufacturing

Companies that have gained experience in international markets may want to build local manufacturing facilities. Local investment in a foreign country may be required to avoid high tariffs, transportation costs, legal problems, and political considerations. Local investment can create a favorable image in the host country while securing better relationships with governments, customs officials, local suppliers, and distributors. This is especially important in industrial markets where reliability of suppliers is an important factor in maintaining a dependable operation.

Cheaper labor or materials may be another reason to invest in a foreign country, although it should not be your only one. For example, in 1983, Nicolas G. Hayek, as head of Swatch, took two major Swiss watchmakers from an unprofitable situation to a profitable one. In the early 1980s, conventional wisdom was to seek low-cost production by manufacturing in countries with low-cost labor. Hayek bucked the trend and retained the manufacturing capabilities in Switzerland, a country with one of the highest labor costs in the world. The expertise and the know-how of the Swiss outweighed the advantage of the lower foreign labor cost.

Before you invest in a foreign country, you need to consider its political and economical stability. Following the departure of the Shah of Iran, many foreign companies in that country were taken over by the government. Local inflation or fluctuation in foreign currency could reverse favorable labor costs.

8.7 Joint ventures

A joint venture is a form of shared ownership and control by companies from different countries. In a joint venture, each company can gain access to a partner's distribution system, technology, managerial capabilities, and capital. Most companies would like to wholly own the partner for reasons of control. Inefficiencies in operations may arise if responsibilities have not been well defined. Joint ventures should be formed for mutual benefit between companies that have common goals and are willing to share responsibilities.

Joint venture partners can offer important skills or market contacts. In some countries, governments may insist on joint ownership as a condition of entry. In developing countries with limited access to supplies and technological know-how, a joint venture may be formed to supply only local domestic demand.

Recently, some companies have joined forces to form strategic alliances. AT&T once formed an alliance with Olivetti to share technological knowledge on computers and telecommunications. Alliances can also be formed to improve production efficiency or increase your distribution base.

9. Global Management

Perhaps the greatest pitfall in foreign business ventures is arrogance and naivete. Managers must have open minds to translate ideas or principles to fit local circumstances. "Think globally; act locally" means having a global vision with local identities.

An organization should strive to provide a mission statement that binds the fabric and shared values of the company. Your mission statement, while providing direction, needs to respect individual diversity and cultural differences. People generally look for structure but not imposed authority.

The best product with the right marketing campaign will not succeed without commitment from local personnel. Forced compliance destroys the commitment needed to implement a company's strategies.

We often hear about successful foreign ventures but little about those that fail. The following section covers the common pitfalls.

9.1 Pitfalls

(a) Poor market understanding — a lack of market research in media usage, consumer preferences, established competitors, distribution structures, and government positions.

(b) Inadequate management input — input not sought from subsidiary; rigid business and management practices from the home office; failure to institute local pride and ownership or autonomy.

(c) Marketing standardization — insistence on product standardization and uniform promotional campaigns.

(d) Poor follow-up — poor communication and reporting systems; failure to monitor progress; failure to share solutions and success stories with other subsidiary.

(e) Diluted resources — deviated from core's competence; trying to please everyone.

9.2 Looking through a window, not a mirror

A product has symbolic value for individuals. It must elicit a need that is consistent with their cultural views. When conducting business in another country, it is important to understand the local infrastructure, customs, language, and behavior. Decision making on a global basis requires you to view things from the perspective of the host country.

18
LEGAL CONSIDERATIONS

There are many legal considerations to marketing a product. Wherever you fit in the distribution chain, from manufacturer, wholesaler, distributor or agent to retailer or salesperson, there is potential product liability. This chapter discusses general legal issues relating to product liability and how to minaimize risk with insurance and control measures. Product liability law, however, differs among jurisdictions. If you run into a problem, do not hesitate to seek professional legal advice. To avoid problems, see a lawyer from the outset.

This book does not deal with protection of patents, copyright, trademarks, and trade names, which are all issues that may affect you if you are a manufacturer. If you want advice or legal help on these issues, you should contact a lawyer. You can also refer to *Take Your Invention to Market*, another book published by Self-Counsel Press.

1. Product Liability

1.1 Contract liability

The term "contract liability" describes any claims made against you alleging breach of the terms of a written, verbal, or implied contract. Breaches could include a sales representative misrepresenting your product, promotional literature stating inaccurate or misleading data, or your failure to meet standards of legislation imposing warranties or obligations of safety and merchantability.

For the claim against you to succeed, it must be proven that —

(a) there was a contract between you and the customer,

(b) you materially failed to perform your obligations under the contract, and

(c) the customer suffered financial or other damages as a result of your breach of contract.

If a customer brings an action against you for a breach of contract, it is irrelevant in most jurisdictions whether the breach was innocent, negligent, or willful. The customer need only prove that a material breach of contract occurred and that damages resulted.

1.2 Tort liability

Tort liability is a violation of civil law rather than a breach of contract. Liability in tort is incurred toward the public at large and generally involves the issue of negligence. Any third party who has suffered through a direct or indirect effect of the product can make a claim for damages against one or possibly all those involved in the distribution chain.

For a person to succeed in a lawsuit against you, he or she must prove that —

(a) you owed the claimant a duty of care,

(b) the duty and/or standard of care required was breached,

(c) measurable financial damages resulted from the breach, and

(d) there was a direct causal connection between the breach of duty and/or standard of care and the damages that occurred.

In a lawsuit based on tort, evidence is introduced into court to establish that you deviated from the standard or duty that was reasonable in the circumstances; in other words, that you did not take reasonable care in designing, producing, or marketing the product.

The courts ask the following questions when determining whether negligence occurred:

(a) Were steps taken to test the product and detect the defect?

(b) Was industry custom complied with?

(c) Were state-of-the-art quality control, product design, and product safety research procedures adopted?

(d) Did the manufacturer have knowledge about product risks that an expert in the industry ought to have known?

(e) Were adequate investments undertaken in product research and development? Were they related to knowledge of and reduction in product risks?

(f) Who were the expected or foreseeable product users?

(g) What was the probability of the risk of personal injury or property damage occurring?

(h) What information did the manufacturer provide to minimize risk of personal injury or property damage?

(i) What cautions did the manufacturer give?

(j) What was the degree to which the risk of physical injury or property damage was obvious to product users?

(k) What was the nature and severity of potential injuries?

(l) Was there compliance with or breach of statutory or regulatory standards?

(m) Did the consumer have the ability to take preventive measures to reduce the risk?

(n) Was it economically feasible for the defendant to undertake accident prevention measures?

(o) What were the terms of the manufacturer's contract with its wholesalers, distributors, or agents?

If you are found to be negligent, the court will attempt to compensate the claimant for the damages incurred. In extreme cases, the courts may also award "punitive damages" as a punishment or warning to others.

1.3 Strict liability

Strict liability contends that a manufacturer is strictly liable in tort rather than liability being dependent on proof of negligence as discussed in the previous section. For example, if a manufacturer places an item on the market that it knows will be used without having been inspected for defects, and that item proves to have a defect, the strict liability doctrine says that the manufacturer is automatically liable. There are exceptions to the application of this legal doctrine, of course, and it is not as widely applied in Canada as it is in the United States. Again, because of the potential risk, it is important to get legal advice in advance.

2. Product Liability Insurance

To avoid lawsuits and to protect yourself financially in case you do lose a lawsuit, you should consider product liability insurance.

2.1 Product liability coverage

Product liability insurance is either included in a comprehensive general liability policy or covered separately. It covers liability arising out of defects in products manufactured, distributed, handled, or sold. Specialty insurance coverage is also available. All liability policies contain the following sections: declarations, exclusions, insuring agreements, definitions, limits of liability, deductibles, and conditions.

2.2 Completed operations liability coverage

Completed operations liability coverage deals with liability from faults in work completed by or for the insured. It is frequently included in policies that are designed for specific industries or businesses.

2.3 Claims made versus occurrence coverage

A claims made policy insures only against claims made during the policy period. Occurrence coverage provides protection against liability occurring during the policy period, even if the claims arise long after the occurrence and after the policy period has passed. The critical point is that the insurance policy has to have been maintained. If it lapses, then no coverage is available.

Claims made policies are generally less costly than occurrence policies because the claims made policy covers only claims made during the policy term. The risk to the insurance company is therefore less, compared to occurrence coverage.

Higher premiums for occurrence coverage reflect the increased risk the insurer assumes for this coverage since a claim can be made against the insurance company many years after the negligence occurred. The cost of settling a claim long after the event could be much higher than making a settlement when the negligence occurred.

2.4 Declarations

The declarations section of an insurance policy contains information about the risk that you are insuring: name, address, policy period, limits of liability, a description of the insured's business, and the name and address of the insurer. It is of the utmost importance that they are correctly completed and that all companies or individuals to be insured are specifically named. This includes both holding companies and subsidiaries that could be included in a legal action.

2.5 Exclusions

Many people feel that insurance companies insert exclusions in a policy to avoid paying claims. This may occasionally be true, but exclusions are also there for other reasons. They protect the insurance company if the risk turns out to be illegal or against public policy, if the risk is or can be insured under another kind of policy, if the risk is too high for the insurance company, or if the exclusion will significantly reduce the cost of the policy.

Products liability insurance is subject to the same exclusions as most liability policies, including the exclusion of damage to property in the care, custody, or control of the insured; liability assumed under contract except for a warranty of goods or products; and obligations under workers' compensation legislation. The following are some of the most common exclusions.

2.5.a Contractual exclusion

Product liability often arises through an implied warranty that the goods or products will be suitable and safe for their intended purposes. Because this is a form of contractual liability, it is essential that every policy provide coverage for liability assumed in a warranty of goods or products.

You must establish whether the basic insuring agreement covers liability assumed under contract. If it doesn't, no matter what the rest of the policy says, contractual liability claims will not be covered. Assuming that there is coverage for contractual liability in the insuring agreements, look carefully at the exclusions. It is very common to find a complete exclusion of all liability assumed under contract, except a contract as defined. Then you have to look in the contract definition section to determine if there is coverage for liability under a warranty of goods or products, whether or not in writing.

2.5.b Business risk

The business risk section is intended to exclude business commitments within the control of an insured. The purpose of this exclusion is to prohibit claims arising from lack of proper performance. For example, if a manufacturer was delayed in completing a contract to produce specialized equipment, and if the delay resulted in a financial loss to a customer's business, the policy would not cover the loss.

This exclusion also applies to claims arising from failure of the insured's products or work performed to meet agreed-upon standards of fitness, quality, performance, or durability. It is assumed that the acceptance of this type of warranty is within the manufacturer's knowledge and control. For example, if a manufacturer warrants that a metal it produces is 100 percent pure, but it is not, and somebody suffers economic loss because of it, that risk is excluded from coverage.

2.5.c Product damage

The replacement of defective products, whether they result in other damage or not, is generally considered to be a trading risk and is not normally insurable. If a single defective appliance is returned, it is not a major problem. This exclusion clause is more important when many products are defective, as with the braking system of a popular car model, for example, or if a small part of a large building is defective and results in damage to the entire structure.

2.5.d Products withdrawal

A products withdrawal clause excludes claims that might be made by a dealer for the costs of withdrawing, repairing, or replacing defective products.

2.6 Insuring agreements

Insuring agreements describe the coverage provided and are divided into three sections. The first deals with the insurer's obligation to pay bodily injury claims on behalf of the insured, the second manages property damage claims, and the third handles the insurer's obligation to investigate and defend.

2.7 Definitions

Most policies contain definitions of product and hazards. Many products, particularly liquids and gases, are supplied in refillable containers which may continue to be the vendor's property and which can be returned to the supplier for reuse. For example, injuries arising out of defective soft drink bottles while they are away from the insured's premises are normally considered product liability claims. Liability from rented or leased equipment does not usually fall within product coverage, as liability is specifically excluded from the definition of products used by many insurers.

As a general rule, two conditions must be present for a loss to qualify under the products liability section of a policy. First, the injury or damage must occur away from the premises of the insured and, second, physical possession must have been relinquished. For example, if a customer was injured on a retailer's premises due to a defective appliance, the loss would not be considered as a products claim. However, should the customer take the appliance home on trial without purchasing it, the same injuries would be considered a products liability claim.

2.8 Limits of liability

Two types of limits appear in liability policies. The first is called "split limits" and the second is called "inclusive limits." Under split limits, a separate limit of liability is applicable for injury to one person, injury to two or more persons, and property damage. With inclusive limits, there is a single amount of insurance for bodily injury and property damage arising out of one occurrence.

Most policies contain an annual aggregate limit on products liability exposure. These limits exist because insurers are concerned about a buildup of losses due to a production run or defective batch which could cause many injuries or claims.

A company manufacturing high volumes of a product that could potentially cause death, injuries, or damage should have substantial limits for bodily injury and property damage. These limits should take into account not only today's estimated cost of settlement, but also inflationary growth or claims escalation between the date of the occurrence and the time when a loss may be settled.

2.9 Deductibles

When a claim is made against your policy, you often have to pay the first portion, or the deductible, of the settlement before the insurance company pays. This is meant to act as an incentive for you to conduct your business affairs carefully. The greater the deductible, the less expensive the policy premium should be.

2.10 Conditions

Products liability insurance applies to bodily injury or property damage that happens during the policy period. In other words, the policy must be in force at the time of the bodily injury or property damage.

The territorial scope of products liability insurance varies and in some cases is restricted to the United States and Canada. In other cases it is worldwide but often subject to a requirement that any claim be brought within the United States or Canada. This limited worldwide extension is of value to a North American manufacturer whose products are only sold in North America but could be carried out of the country. Any company that is manufacturing or selling products in markets outside of the United States or Canada should ensure that the policy covers accidents and lawsuits anywhere in the world.

3. Special Insurance

Although specialty coverage is often costly and difficult to arrange, it may be necessary since there are some risk areas that are not covered by standard products liability insurance.

3.1 Product mixing

Certain products may in themselves be safe, but if accidentally mixed with another product, they may become unusable. For example, a mixture of vegetable seeds may be of little concern to the home gardener, but may present a serious problem for a farmer with 1,000 acres of market produce and $250,000 in automated harvesting equipment that is unusable because of a mixed crop. Or, if a large dairy's daily production of milk is accidentally mixed with green food coloring, it may do no nutritional harm, but would still render the product unmarketable.

3.2 Product withdrawal

The cost of withdrawing widely distributed products of a hazardous nature from the market can be enormous. For example, the cost of withdrawing flammable textiles or defective cars or airplanes is almost beyond comprehension.

Understandably, then, there are few insurance companies who insure the cost of withdrawing defective products from the market. The premiums and deductible amount would be extremely high considering the risk.

3.3 Product damage

Product damage coverage is of little importance to the manufacturer with a small output of relatively low-value products, but it can present a massive liability exposure to a contractor who may at any time be held liable for the destruction of an entire building.

3.4 Product failure

Product failure coverage addresses risks excluded by the business risk exclusion. It protects a manufacturer for the failure of a product and covers any loss to the customer. The product must fail to perform the function intended, and the failure must be due to a mistake or deficiency in any design, formula, or plan prepared by the manufacturer.

3.5 Product extortion

Product extortion coverage is designed to protect an insured from loss due to an extortion attempt based on a threatened risk. A threat to poison a food or medication product would be covered under this type of insurance.

3.6 Professional liability

Many firms sell custom, specialty, and prototype products which may prove to be improperly designed and may result in losses to a customer where there is no bodily injury or damage to property. In addition, the consequent loss may be excluded by the business risk exclusion. A good example is a computer firm selling both software and hardware. You may wish to have professional liability insurance in this type of situation.

4. Doing Business Without Insurance

Some people choose to conduct their business without any product liability insurance. If the degree of exposure and risk is very low, this might be a viable alternative, especially if you operate an incorporated company with limited assets. But in certain cases you may be required to have product liability insurance or others will not distribute, represent, or sell your product. If you intend to operate without product liability insurance, it is important that you receive expert legal advice.

5. Loss Prevention

Loss prevention describes a deliberate plan for avoiding or minimizing potential legal problems. It is an ongoing process with specially designed systems that should commence during initial product planning and continue through the manufacturing, testing, distributing, operating and marketing stages, the sale of the product, and after-sale follow-up.

At the presale stage, for example, you need to consider industry standards, mandatory regulations, adequate instructional material, and product warranties. During the distribution stage, a manufacturer must consider the standards required for dealer training, customer education and feedback, product modification, product recall, and product withdrawal.

To ensure that you have optimal coverage for the risks that you may be exposed to and the premiums that you can afford, be certain that you receive quotations from at least three insurance brokers. Insurance brokers can be found in the Yellow Pages or may be recommended by your industry or trade association. Once you have finalized your choice, have a lawyer who specializes in insurance law review the policy.

Appendix 1
RESEARCHING YOUR MARKET

Many people shy away from research because they think it requires complex statistical analysis. For most situations, all you need is the willingness to listen, an open mind, and the ability to put aside any personal bias or preconceived ideas.

1. What You Need To Know

Market research can help you determine:

- who your market is,
- who your customer is, and
- how effective you are in satisfying your customer needs.

1.1 Who is your market?

How well do you know your market? Are your products targeted to certain age or gender groups? Is your market a specialty market with few competitors or is your market a mass market with many competitors? Are your products or services priced the same as your competitors or do you offer specialty products that are not widely distributed? Is your market area limited to a certain geographic area or do customers come from a wide area to buy your products or services? Can you differentiate your product or service on the basis of price, quality, or service?

1.2 Who is your customer?

How well do you know your customer? Are they mostly male or female? Are they under or over 40? Are they professionals, construction workers, or senior citizens? Do they make repeat purchases or buy your products or services at certain times of the year? Do they live in a certain area? Do they have similar educational backgrounds, income levels, or interests?

1.3 Are you satisfying your customers' needs?

How well are you satisfying your customers' needs? More important, how well are you satisfying your customers' needs compared to your competitors? Customers can choose from a wide variety of businesses to buy similar products or services. A customer service program that encourages repeat and loyal customers is more profitable in the long run than one that is made up of mostly new or nonrepeat customers.

2. Why Market Research?

Market research helps formalize answers to questions about your market, your customers, and your customer service program. Market research can be as simple as asking a customer about how he or she was served today or as complex as hiring a professional market research company.

Most businesses know a great deal about their customers or their market. Typically, businesses use sales records, look at competitors' advertising, or factor in such variables as the weather or how the economy is doing to help them make business decisions.

Rarely do businesses talk to their customers about what is important. Salespeople are trained to find out what a customer wants in the way of product features or benefits or price. But how often do you or your salespeople ask the customer what is important?

2.1 The customer

The customer is the most important part of the selling process. Nothing can be sold until a customer is ready to buy. The more you know about your customer, your market, and the service level required, the more sales your business will have. Getting to know your customers is easy. Talk to them. This sounds simplistic, yet most businesses don't do it.

The best way to get customers to talk to you is to approach them before they come into your place of business or after they leave.

2.2 Talking to your customer before a sale is made

Do you know why a customer comes to your business to purchase a product or service? Do you know why potential customers don't purchase from you? Do you know how many potential customers are aware of your business, your products, or services? By talking to customers and potential customers before they come into your business, you can find out answers to the above questions.

If you have a customer list, phone or write to 10 to 20 of your customers. Make a list of questions you want to ask them. For example, what do they know, not know, like, or dislike about your business, your products, your service, your staff, and your pricing program? The fact that you took the time to call or write to these customers shows you are interested in them and value their opinions.

Ask them if they would provide you with a list of their friends, neighbors, or relatives who may not be aware of your business and compile a set of questions to ask these non-customers.

2.3 Talking to your customer after a sale is made

Research has shown that most customers who receive poor service do not return to that store or business. Successful businesses rely on loyal, repeat customers.

Talking to your customers after a sale is made helps you find out how loyal your customers are. Do they like your staff, your location, your hours of business, and your selection of products and services? Are they aware of the extra service features you provide? Do they tell their neighbors or friends about their shopping experience at your place of business? More important, how does your business compare to that of your competitors in terms of price, service, selection, quality, and value?

If you are serious about talking to your customers, take the time to write down a list of questions that compares your business with your competitors'. Phone your recent customers and ask them how the service was. How attentive were you to their needs? Was your pricing fair and competitive? Based on their experience, did they find your products, services, prices, and quality to be better than the competition, equal, or worse?

3. Developing a Market Research Program

The first step in developing a market research program begins with the belief that what the customer wants is important. If you are not prepared to listen to your customer and act on his or her needs, market research is wasted time and money.

However, if you are serious about listening to your customer, market research can help you increase sales and differentiate your business from your competitors.

How you develop a market research program depends on the time and financial resources you have available. What is more important is to develop and implement a plan of action that covers the following steps.

(a) List your market research objectives.

(b) Write down the questions or information you need answers to.

(c) Survey your customers.

(d) Analyze the results.

(e) Implement changes in response to customer needs.

Look at the example below:

> A specialty clothing retailer has opened a second store in a new location, but after two years of being open, the average customer sale at the new store is 30 percent less than the average customer sale at the first store.

The five steps that follow show how you can develop a market research program for your business.

3.1 Market research objective

Your market research objectives should be simple and specific. They should relate to the questions or problems you are seeking answers or information to.

Take a few moments and think about a market research objective for your business. It may have something to do with your customer service program, information about your customers, the effectiveness of your advertising program, or whether you should expand to a new location. Write down the objective(s) below.

Objective 1

_____

_____

_____

Objective 2

_____

_____

_____

Objective 3

_____

_____

_____

3.2 Questions and information worksheet

Now that you have listed your objectives, think about specific questions or information to which you would like to have answers. Write down as many questions as you want and then prioritize the five most important questions. If you have more than five priority questions, separate these into two lists. The most important list of questions is your "must know" list. Call the second list your "nice to know" list.

In the example of the specialty clothing retailer, we determined our market research objective: to find out why the average customer sale for the new store is 30 percent less than the average customer sale for the first store.

To find the solution, we need answers to the following questions:

1. Are the customer profiles different between the two stores?

2. Are there other specialty stores offering similar products located near the new store?

3. Are there customer service problems associated with the new store?

4. Should the product mix be different for each store?

5. Is the pricing program causing for the lower per customer sale at the new store?

Think about the market research objective(s) you wrote down for your own business. Write down a list of questions you would need to ask customers.

Most often the questions should deal with your market, your customer, and customer satisfaction.

Question 1

_____

_____

_____

Question 2

_____

_____

_____

Question 3

_____

_____

_____

Question 4

_____

_____

_____

Question 5

_____

_____

_____

3.3 Surveying your customer

Finding out answers to your questions involves surveying your customers. How you survey your customers depends on how much time and money you want to spend.

Generally, surveys take one of two forms. With the written survey, you have customers complete questions in person or over the telephone. With the personal survey, you informally ask questions of people individually or as a group.

For most small businesses with limited resources and time, customer surveys should be made as quickly and easily as possible.

3.3.a Written survey

The written survey involves having customers complete answers to questions either in person, in your store, or over the telephone. The advantage of the written survey is that it provides you with specific answers to your questions.

Written surveys should typically have between 20 to 100 completed questionnaires. If you are using the telephone, provide a brief explanation about why you are doing the survey.

3.3.b Personal survey

The personal survey is more general and involves talking personally with customers. It allows you to probe into certain issues. In some cases, you may want to invite 8 to 10 of your customers to a round-table discussion. Have a broad outline of the issues you want answers and comments on.

Using our specialty store example, the surveying approach would be to develop a written survey based on the five questions we developed and to then call between 20 to 50 customers of the new store.

Using your own objective and questions, decide which survey format would be best for you (you may want to use both).

Now determine —

- how many customers you want to talk to,
- when you want to call them,
- how you want to talk to them (i.e., telephone survey, individual survey, group discussion), and
- the exact questions you want to ask them.

3.4 Analyzing the results

Once you complete your survey, it is important to analyze the results. If you talked to more than 20 people, you may want to tabulate or summarize the results for each question.

For example:

- 30 percent of the customers felt the customer service was poor.
- 55 percent of the customers felt the prices were too high compared to other stores.
- 73 percent of the customers like the selection and variety of merchandise.

If you talked with fewer than ten people, review their individual comments and form some general impressions. For example: "I really like your service. Your staff goes out of their way to help me find the right size and style." Or, "I feel your prices are too high. I can buy the same item for 20 percent less at the competition."

3.5 Implement change

Implementing change is the end result of any market research program. Perhaps your service levels are below your competitions' or customers aren't aware of your location and hours of business.

Involve your staff in the research process; they are a critical part in implementing changes.

After you have made changes, follow up with your customers to see how you are doing. Find out if they are aware of the changes you have made.

By constantly talking to your customers, you can fine-tune your marketing program. Talking to your customers also gives you an ongoing market research program.

4. Forecasting

Forecasting sales revenue is too often a process of a wish, a hope, and a prayer. Many businesses spend little time forecasting next year's or next month's revenue. Those that do forecast typically look at last year's sales revenue and inflate it by 5 to 10 percent to cover increased prices and sales growth.

Forecasting revenue is an important part of the planning process. As such, forecasting deserves more time than completing a one-page summary of your last year's sales and factoring in how much more you plan on selling next year.

Accurate forecasting involves a thorough understanding of where your sales are coming from. What products are selling and which ones are not? What time of year are products selling? Are they seasonal products? Are they affected by special sales programs or advertising programs?

Accurate forecasting also involves knowing your customers. What are their buying patterns? How do they react to your sales programs?

As we saw in Chapter 5, knowing your customers is important in order to respond to their needs. By doing research on customer needs, businesses can also use that information to help them in their sales forecasting.

For example, if the market research shows that customers prefer sales at certain times of the year and that sales typically increase revenue by 30 percent to 40 percent, then the forecasting would take into account the planning of sales for certain times and the additional revenue to be received from those sales.

Linking your market research program to your forecasting is a circular process. By constantly talking to your customers about what is important to them, you are in the enviable position of being able to constantly fine-tune your sales and marketing program to take advantage of what your customers are telling you.

The more you respond to your customer needs, the more sales you should have and the more important forecasting those sales becomes.

To illustrate, let's suppose that your last year's sales revenue was $600,000 and was equally divided between three products: A, B, and C.

4.1 Research results

After completing a market research survey of your customers, you determined that for:

- Product A: 20 percent of your customers regularly purchased this product as a treat when coming in to buy other products,

- Product B: 60 percent of your customers purchased this product after they were made aware of it, and

- Product C: 65 percent of your customers indicated that they bought this product from you because it was priced far below (20 percent) comparable products at competing stores.

4.2 Assumptions

Based on the information provided through the market research, a reasonable forecast for next year for products A, B, and C would be as follows:

- Product A: Past records indicate that under normal economic conditions, sales revenue increases at the same rate as the population. The forecast for population growth in your area says that the population is expected to increase by 2 percent for next year. Economic conditions are expected to remain the same.

- Product B: Records indicate that sales revenue went up by 10 percent as a result of two three-month advertising campaigns. You plan to have two more advertising campaigns for next year.

- Product C: After talking to your customers, you deduce that a price increase of 5 percent would increase your sales without losing your customers.

4.3 Forecast

Last year's sales revenue

Product A	$100,000
Product B	$150,000
Product C	$200,000
Total sales	$450,000

Next year's sales revenue

Product A	$102,000 ($100,000 x 2%)
Product B	$165,000 ($150,000 x 10%)
Product C	$210,000 ($200,000 x 5%)
Total forecast sales	$477,000

Worksheet 2 on the following page can help you use your research results to make sales forecasts.

For more information on market research, see *Market Research Made Easy*, another title published by Self-Counsel Press.

WORKSHEET 2
FORECASTING DEMAND FROM RESEARCH RESULTS

1. Summarize your research results:

   1. Customer survey

   2. Past records

   3. Industry growth

      Economic and trends

      Competitive actions

2. Identify forecast assumptions for each product:

   Product A

   Product B

   Product C

3. Write last year's revenue

Product A	$_____
Product B	_____
Product C	_____
Total	$_____

4. Write next year's revenue

Product A	$_____
Product B	_____
Product C	_____
Total	$_____

Appendix 2
THE MARKETING PLAN

The extent to which this plan is relevant to your needs dictates what parts you may wish to complete.

1. Title page

The title page is the first thing readers see. It should give a positive appearance. Ensure the title page information is clear and visible. The title page should contain the following information:

- Product name
- Time period
- Person(s) and position(s) submitting the plan
- Date of submission

2. Executive Summary

The executive summary should be an action-oriented summary that presents a two- to three-page overview of the marketing plan for quick skimming. It should begin with a brief introduction to the company and the product, and follow with the key components of your plan, including the following:

- Customer awareness of your product
- Expected market share
- Means of distribution
- Communication strategy
- Expected budget and timing

- Relative profit potential
- Money required to implement the plan
- Conclusion

The following is an example of a summary where product differentiation is the goal of the market plan.

Product differentiation

We will position our product by providing superior product quality or unique features or services. Quality, features, or service should be briefly described. Decrease the number of products returned because of defects by 10 percent in the first year and 15 percent in the second year.

Distribution accessibility

We will make our product available to all mass merchandising stores through the West or only to specialized service retail outlets in cities with more than 100,000 in population.

Promotion strategy

We intend to use mixed media such as television combined with a heavy sampling that will reach 40 percent of all residents within city X.

Pricing strategy

We will charge five percent below or above the industry leader.

3. Table of Contents

The table of contents should list all the main elements of the marketing plan including charts and figures.

4. Introduction

The introduction should tell readers what the report is about and discuss the current marketing situation in terms of product, competition, and distribution. The following information should be present.

4.1 Existing product

Describe briefly the background and history of the business and product. Show sales, profits, and market shares for the past three to five years. Explain reasons for change and what changes are proposed.

4.2 New product

Product concept give reasons why you believe it will be successful. Give estimates of sales levels, costs, and returns on investment.

5. Situational Analysis

The situational analysis enumerates the relevant environmental factors that affect the chances of success or failure for your product. The analysis should consider the effect of the following factors:

- Structure of the industry and nature of competition
- Trends and growth potential of the industry
- Economic conditions and relevant economic factors
- Social change and population shift relevant to your business
- Political and legislative action that may alter the way you do business
- Regulations that may have an impact on your business
- Major suppliers

6. Competitive Analysis

The competitive analysis should determine the relative strengths and weaknesses of your major competitors. The analysis should address the following issues:

- Identify the main competitor within your market
- The key firms' financial positions and marketing capabilities
- Competitors' strengths and weaknesses
- Market strategies employed by your competitors
- Your market share
- Likelihood of new competitor entry
- How your competitors react to changes
- How you compare with your competitors

7. Target Market

The target market should provide a description of your customers and the benefits they want. Research such as focus group sessions, surveys, questionnaires, or talking with your customers, wholesalers, retailers, and suppliers will help you determine answers to the following questions:

- What is the market size and area you intend to serve?
- What are the needs of your customers?
- What are the leading benefits your product provides?
- What is the current level of awareness about your product?
- How many customers purchase and use the product?
- Give an overall description of your customer in terms of relevant demographics and psychographics to your product.
- Describe heavy users versus light users.
- Where do customers currently purchase the product?

- How much are they willing to pay?
- What media reach these customers?
- What purchasing trends may affect the availability of your product?
- What are the benefits sought by the customer?
- Are the benefits functional, social, or psychological?

8. Marketing Objectives

The marketing objectives should state the expected outcomes in percentages or volumes. Objectives should at least include sales volume, market share, profit margin, and the four Ps.

Set Product Objectives

Incorporate our enhanced graphics printing capabilities by next year.

Reduce packaging cost from $3.50 to $3.20 for department stores. Model A and B will receive 80 percent of the marketing dollars due to high profit margin.

Set Promotion Objectives

Increase awareness (or recognition) of brand X from 20 percent to 35 percent among all seniors in City A. Demonstrate our new tool kit to 350 contractors.

Set Place Objectives

Develop in-store merchandising units to demonstrate product features. Expand distribution among chains from 20 percent to 35 percent among independent retail outlets and from 15 percent to 25 percent in department stores.

Set Price Objectives

Increase price on luxury model from $55.50 to $75.50.

9. Market Strategies

The market strategy explains how you intend to meet your marketing objectives. The means by which you can meet your marketing objectives depend on how you manage your marketing mix. Your marketing mix should look at the four following areas:

(a) Product: Describe how your product differs from the competition. Will you provide more features, different styles, or give longer warranties?

(b) Promotion: Describe how you will communicate the major benefits or how your brand differs from the competition. Will you do special deals, coupons, point-of-purchase, or advertising? Will you use audio or print advertising? Will you use a long message or a short reminder?

(c) Distribution: Describe how you will increase your market coverage. Will you use selective exposure or a mass retailer? Will you use your own sales force? Will you use advertising as a pull or push strategy?

(d) Price: Describe reasons for using cost-plus pricing or demand pricing. Explain reasons for special deals, discounts, or sales commission levels and its effect on sales volumes and profits.

10. Customer Service

Customer service includes all services that are provided in addition to your product. Your sales force as well as all personnel in the company should be part of the service link. In a competitive environment, service may be the best way to distinguish yourself from your competitors. Set objectives for the performance of customer service. For example:

- All phones will be answered by the third ring.

- All personnel will have access to all marketing information about the product.

- Service required from technical personnel will be provided within one work day.

Objectives should also be set for your sales force. For example, you might set the following objectives:

- Maintain the current sales force of 15 people and increase sales in the first year to $2,100,000 from $2,000,000.

- Lower cost of service for each sales call from $35 to $30.

- Increase the average sales closing ratio from 20 percent to 25 percent.

Improvement in sales force productivity should also include a plan on how this will be accomplished. A productivity improvement plan might include the following:

- Increased sales will be accomplished by installing a toll-free telephone number line to help customer tracking.

- Lower costs will be obtained through computer automation of the ordering process.

- A bonus system based on profit will be instituted.

- A five-day training session will be provided to all sales personnel on closing techniques.

11. Sales Forecast

Your sales forecast might include the following:

- Forecast sales per month up to one year

- Give sales forecast assumptions

- Provide an assessment of critical risk factors, such as possible strike action against the company, suppliers, or loss of key employees

12. Action Plan

An action plan is the execution of the strategies. The plan should clearly spell out who does what, when, and how much will be spent. The action plan requires careful scheduling and attention to detail. The following questions need to be answered:

- Who is responsible for implementing and controlling the marketing plan?

- What tasks must be performed?

- Who is responsible for each task?

- What are the deadlines for each task?

- What are the costs for each task?

- How will you measure success or failure?

- What is the expected time needed for results?

- What needs to happen before you alter the plan?

BONUS CD-ROM

This book comes with a bonus CD-ROM that includes extra advertising information, a glossary, a bibliography, and the following forms. The forms were prepared by marketing specialist Aaron Morris and are provided by Self-Counsel Press.

Form	1	General Objectives
Form	2	Benefits and Features
Form	3	Judging the Competition
Form	4	Analysis of the Competition
Form	5	Target Market Analysis
Form	6	Costing
Form	7	Marketing and Promotion
Form	8	Sales Analysis
Form	9	Outside Influences
Form	10	Outside Influences — P.E.S.T.
Form	11	Internal Influences — S.W.O.T.
Form	12	Forecasting for the Future
Form	13	Industry Trends
Form	14	Personal and Professional Objectives
Form	15	Company Objectives
Form	16	Product and Brand Extension
Form	17	Markcting Budget — Yearly
Form	18	Advertising Calendar
Form	19	Activities and Budgets
Form	20	Trade Show Analysis
Form	21	Test Market Your Product
Form	22	Product Survey
Form	23	Marketing Plan

The following worksheets are also included on the bonus CD-ROM and were provided by Donald Cyr and Douglas Gray.

Worksheet 1	Assessing the Competition
Worksheet 2	Forecasting Demand from Research Results
Worksheet 3	Advertising